TRUMPED

THE SILENT VOTERS SPEAK

BILL G. MARKS

authorHOUSE®

AuthorHouse™
1663 Liberty Drive
Bloomington, IN 47403
www.authorhouse.com
Phone: 1 (800) 839-8640

Published by AuthorHouse 05/12/2017

ISBN: 978-1-5246-9171-4 (sc)
ISBN: 978-1-5246-9170-7 (e)

DEDICATION

This book is dedicated to my wonderful wife of 51 years, Marion, and our three children and their families: Thomas, Michael, and Diane. You have brought much joy and happiness to my life.

I would like to make a special dedication to my only sister, Joan Marks Yearwood, who died in December, 2016 and my brother, Jack Marks, who also passed away in June, 2016. A special thanks to my father, J. B. Marks, Jr. and my mother, Hautense Fisher Marks for being wonderful parents.

As in my first book, *The Other Side of the Law,* no comment or expression within the text refers to my wife or her family or any other persons except those mentioned in this book, which is strictly about the 2016 presidential election, the candidates involved and those involved in reporting, analyzing, commenting on it or are otherwise involved in the election.

ACKNOWLEDGEMENTS

This book could not have been written without the assistance and encouragement of my wife, Marion, who made many insightful and wise suggestions to improve this book. Thank you for your dedicated efforts. It's great to be married to an English major.

I am fortunate to be a member of the Writers' Bloc Club in my community. They critiqued several of the chapters in this book and made many creative and helpful suggestions. I thank you for your kind assistance and wisdom.

Since the summer of 2015, I have talked to many people about this election, and speaking confidentially, they have expressed how they felt about the various candidates running for president. After each party selected their nominee, many told me how they felt about Hillary Clinton and Donald Trump. I promised to keep their statements made to me confidential, so I will not reveal any names, but I am deeply grateful to them for their willingness to talk to me. They know who they are and I simply say thank you for your help in making this book more interesting.

I want to give a special thanks to Judith Czajkowski who was kind enough to send me valuable information as I was writing this book and for making insightful suggestions along the way, including helping me select an appropriate title. Her creative ideas are much appreciated. She was also kind enough to proofread my manuscript and make helpful suggestions. It's great to have smart friends.

Speaking of smart friends, I would like Will Passmore to know how much I appreciate his efforts in reading my manuscript. Will taught English for 32 years and made many helpful suggestions to improve my book.

Also, I would like to thank June Hagel, who read my manuscript and made numerous creative recommendations to improve on this book.

You may be wondering why I had so many people proofread my manuscript. I have learned from experience that the more people who read the manuscript the better it becomes.

I am grateful to NBC, CBS, ABC, MSNBC, CNN, Fox News, *Wikipedia,* Buzz Feed, *The Washington Post, USA Today, Forbes Magazine,* Bloomberg Network, *Associated Press, Fortune Magazine, Reuters, The New York Political Observer, National Review, Politico Magazine, New York Post, The New York Times and The Wall Street Journal* to name just a few of the sources I used in writing this book. I constantly used these sources and the internet to obtain information.

I would like to thank all the candidates who ran for president in this election. It takes tremendous energy and courage to run for President of the United States. The amount of time spent generally last about a minimum of two years and it can take much longer. Your life becomes a glass house for every voter to look into so they can decide if they want to vote for you. The sacrifice away from family and the day to day pressures are enormous.

I would like to give a special thanks to Donald Trump who gave up running his large business empire so he could run for the office. This was a great sacrifice for him and his family.

Also to Hillary Clinton, I appreciate her time and effort in making her second run for this position. She deserves our appreciation for her dedicated service to our country.

CONTENTS

INTRODUCTION

The Critical Issue

As we approached the presidential election of 2016, it seemed appropriate to ask the critical issue facing the voters in this election: are we going to have a government of the people, by the people and for the people or a government controlled by special interests, lobbyists and power brokers? After talking with many people, it seems average Americans no longer feel that they have much of a say or control over who is elected. It takes so much money to get elected that only the lobbyists, people in charge of PACs, Washington power brokers and extremely wealthy people have a say in who is elected. Thus, our government at this time is no longer of, by or for the people. The question is whether this will change. After the election, it appeared the silent voters spoke and took back control over who was elected.

In regard to the Democrats, we had just learned that the Democratic National Committee (DNC) took certain steps to favor the election of Hillary Clinton over Bernie Sanders. The people in many primaries voted for Bernie over Hillary, but due to the super delegates, Hillary kept on getting more delegates than Bernie. Then, we found out, thanks to WikiLeaks disclosing the DNC emails, the chairman and members of the DNC were taking a course of action that would favor Hillary over Bernie. Bernie's supporters protested at the Democratic convention, causing the DNC Chair to resign on the morning of the beginning of the convention. Debbie Wasserman Schultz had hoped to open the convention, deliver a speech to the delegates, close the convention and then resign. All these plans changed when the DNC emails were disclosed. Ms. Schultz appeared before the Florida delegates on Monday morning, July 25, and was booed off the platform causing her to leave the convention in disgrace. The people who supported Bernie felt cheated and thought that the election of Hillary was rigged by the DNC. It was estimated that approximately 10% of the Bernie supporters would vote for Trump.

In regard to the Republicans, the Republican National Committee (RNC) insisted that Trump sign a loyalty oath promising to vote for the GOP nominee. All 17 candidates signed the oath. At first, Trump refused to sign as he was concerned that he would not be treated fairly by the RNC. He finally agreed to sign after talking to the chairman and being assured that he would, in fact, be treated with respect and fairness. Trump went on the attack against the other candidates and they began dropping out of the race like flies. It appeared that the Republican power brokers, lobbyists and Washington elected officials wanted nothing to do with Trump. He refused to accept large contributions from the lobbyists, so they refused to join him in his efforts to gain the nomination.

There was just one big problem with all this. The people of this country listened to what Trump had to say, and they liked what he said. They showed up in droves at his rallies, and the Republican power brokers watched in shock as the people voted for Trump. The Washington establishment tried every way in the world to defeat him, but they failed in each attempt. The power brokers did not care what the people wanted, but they could not control what the people did, so they lost. Near the end of the primaries there were only three candidates remaining: Trump, Cruz and Kasich. Many of the candidates refused to support Trump, thus breaking their promise. Cruz came and spoke to the convention, but refused to endorse Trump. Kasich refused to endorse Trump and did not come to the convention which was held in the state of Ohio where he currently serves as governor. Bush 41, Bush 43 and Jeb Bush refused to come to the convention and Jeb refused to endorse Trump. It was obvious that the Republicans were split, which could have caused Trump to lose the election.

For the purposes of this book, I referred to Secretary Hillary Clinton as Hillary because her campaign signs used only her first name in their advertising. In turn, I referred to Donald Trump as Trump because his campaign signs used only his last name in their advertising.

I have expressed my personal opinion in several chapters of this book and those opinions are italicized so the reader will be able to distinguish my opinions from other opinions also expressed.

So Many Questions and So Few Answers

Before the election, I talked with a 70 year old friend who told me: "I have no idea who I am going to vote for. I don't like Hillary because I don't trust her, and I don't like Trump because he is so off the wall with many of his comments."

I told him, "Be patient, I believe things will clear up as we get closer to the day of the election."

Two hours later another friend doing work for me around the house came by to complete a project and all of a sudden started talking about the election. He said, "I'm so confused about this political race that I may not vote. I don't believe either Clinton or Trump, and I sure don't believe the press who is supposed to be covering the candidates and giving us the truth about them."

I tried to console him and told him, "You are not alone, but it is early in the election process and hopefully the situation will become better understood as we get closer to November 8, the day of the election.

It was during this same time that I watched a Trump rally being held in Alabama, where about 30,000 supporters showed up to hear Trump speak. A reporter interviewed one of the men in attendance and asked him why he supported Trump. His reply was, "I believe Trump will get more done in a week than Obama and the members of Congress got done in 8 years. I'm ready for a change."

Upon hearing this, I realized that this race could turn out to be a shock to the nation if Trump was victorious because at this point many people thought Hillary was a sure winner.

Why all the confusion? What was going on that was causing all these people to be frustrated and undecided?

The answer I believe is simple. *We have many people who have so many questions and they are not getting satisfactory answers.*

On June 2, 2016, it was five days away from California and five other state primaries and only a little over five months until the day of the election. Would Bernie upset Hillary to destroy her momentum going into the Democratic Convention? Would the super delegates continue to support Hillary? Would Hillary be indicted for obstructing justice in the misuse of her private server while she was Secretary of State? Would Bill and Hillary be indicted for corruption in the use of The Clinton Foundation, where Hillary encouraged a contribution to her foundation from anyone seeking to talk to her as Secretary of State? It was rumored that the FBI had been investigating the Clinton Foundation for several months. Would the Attorney General or President Obama block the indictment if the FBI recommended prosecution? Would the Democrats decide that Hillary is too risky a choice to be the nominee and replace her with Bernie Sanders? Would the Democratic delegates decide to go with Vice President Joe Biden and tell both Hillary and Bernie to get lost? Would Bernie's followers leave the Democratic Party and vote for Trump?

If these questions were not enough to confuse the people, let's not leave out the Republicans. Would Paul Ryan, Bill Kristol and Mitt Romney continue to refuse to support Trump and endorse Bill Lewis or Mitt Romney as an Independent candidate? If there was an Independent Candidate running, no candidate might receive a sufficient number of electors so that the election would be thrown into the House of Representatives. Then what? Would the Republicans try to find a replacement for Trump at the time of their convention, and if so, who would they select? Jeb Bush, Ted Cruz, John Kasich, Marco Rubio or one of the other candidates who ran for the nomination or someone like Mitt Romney who didn't? Would Trump be able to get Latinos, Mexicans and other minorities to vote for him and how would he achieve this? Would Trump change the way women feel and think about him so that they would end up voting for him?

How did this country get in such a political mess? How could we make changes to the election process so that the people actually have a valid say in what happens? Could we overturn the Supreme Court United Citizens case so our elections won't cost so much? Could we limit the amount of money lobbyists donate to candidates so that they are not so obligated to do what the lobbyists want? Do we have the finest politicians money can buy? Can we amend the United States Constitution so term limits are placed on our elected representatives? These are just some of the questions that the people want answered.

The next six months promised an exciting, eventful and historic election. There was a possibility that for the first time we would have a woman heading up a major party ticket, and for the first time, we would have a candidate running in a major party who refused to accept large contributions as he basically self-funds his primary campaign, which the Trump supporters highly approve.

To put all these past, present and future events in perspective, I think it is wise to start at the beginning and provide a chronological summary of the events as they unfolded, so we can see how this election finally plays out. I have chosen to start with the announcement of Hillary Clinton as she decided to run for the presidency once again. After considering the Democratic field, I will address the Republican candidates and then the Libertarian Party.

Hold on tight as this race promises to be a bumpy ride.

CHAPTER 1

The Presidential Announcements And Primaries

The Democrats

On a quiet Sunday afternoon of July 12, 2015, Hillary Clinton announced her run for the presidency by means of a low key video. She chose not to have a large crowd or a live event and down played the announcement. She defended President Obama's healthcare plan, Obamacare, women's equality and talked about restoring the disappearing middle class to a thriving class of people. She told her audience that her campaign was about everyday Americans who were trying to build a better life for themselves and their families. Regarding domestic policy issues, she embraced the overhaul of the tax code and reforming the immigration system. She proposed expansion of the pre-kindergarten education program and a plan to reduce the cost of a college education. On foreign policy issues, she advocated sanctions for Iran and voiced concern over Iran becoming a country having nuclear power.

Hillary became the first Democrat to announce her run for the presidency, and it was expected that Vice President Joe Biden, former Maryland Governor Martin O'Malley, former Virginia Senator Jim Webb, Senator Elizabeth Warren of Massachusetts and Independent Senator Bernie Sanders of Vermont might join in the race for the Democratic nomination.

The great surprise was that Joe Biden's son died of brain cancer and he decided not to run, or could it have been that Biden thought that Hillary would be indicted, and he could step into the Democratic convention and get the nomination without having to campaign for a year? Martin O'Malley barely made a dent in the race and decided to stop his run after a short time. Elizabeth Warren decided not to run. Former Rhode Island Governor Lincoln Chafee and Harvard Law Professor Lawrence Lessig announced as candidates and then disappeared in thin air and that left Vermont Independent Senator Bernie Sanders to figure out if he should run in the Democratic Party. No one ever dreamed that 14 months later Bernie would not only still be in the race, but also driving Hillary crazy, as he had won 21 state primaries to 28 for Hillary. The delegate count was 1775 for Hillary compared to 1502 for Bernie. Hillary had a big lead in super delegates with 523 for her to 46 for Bernie. (The super delegates or unpledged delegates are appointed at the convention by the party, independently of the primary electoral process.) Two days before the California primary Bernie was in a dead heat with Hillary in California, but she needed only 85 more delegates to secure the nomination when unpledged Super delegates were counted. At this point Hillary was 3 million popular votes ahead of Bernie. On June 6, Clinton reached the magic number of 2,383 when the super delegates from Puerto Rico were included.

So it appeared that Hillary would get the nomination, but could it be by this time she might be so damaged that she couldn't win the presidency?

The Republicans

The Republican field opened in March, 2015 and quickly grew to 17 candidates, which added to the complexity and challenges involved in the Republican primary, and, considering Trump's strategy, may have actually been a factor in his ultimate victory. It was the largest presidential primary field for any party in American history and began when Senator Ted Cruz of Texas became the first of 17 candidates to announce his candidacy. Former Governor of Florida Jeb Bush, retired neurosurgeon Ben Carson of Maryland, Governor Chris Christie of New Jersey, businesswoman Carly Fiornia of California, former Governor Jim Gilmore of Virginia, Senator Lindsey Graham of South Carolina, former Governor Mike Huckabee of Arkansas, former Governor Bobby Jindal of Louisiana, Governor John Kasich of Ohio, former Governor George Pataki of New York, Senator

Paul Rand of Kentucky, former Governor Rick Perry of Texas, Senator Marco Rubio of Florida, former Senator Rick Santorum of Pennsylvania, businessman Donald Trump of New York and Governor Scott Walker of Wisconsin rounded out the field.

On June 16, 2015, Trump called a press conference to be held in the lobby of Trump Towers and announced that he was running for President of the United States on the GOP ticket. He announced that he was funding his primary campaign and would not accept large contributions or PAC money as he was worth $8.7 billion dollars. He promised to do away with Obamacare and replace it with a better health care program. He promised to be the greatest jobs president in the history of the USA, saying that we would get jobs back from China, Japan and Mexico. He said a wall would be built at Mexico's expense along our southern border to keep illegal immigrants and drugs from coming into our country. Claiming the American dream was dead, he said he would bring back the dream and make America great again.

It didn't take long for the field to narrow. Prior to the Iowa caucus on February 1, Perry, Walker, Jindal, Graham and Pataki withdrew due to low polling numbers. It's possible that lack of funds also played an important role in these decisions. Cruz won the Iowa caucus with Trump a close second, even though the polls showed Trump leading prior to the vote. Huckabee, Paul and Santorum withdrew due to a poor performance in the Iowa vote. Trump won New Hampshire easily after which Christie, Fiorina and Gilmore bailed out. In the South Carolina primary, Trump, Rubio, Cruz and Bush finished in that order and Bush cut out due to his poor showing in fourth place. On Super Tuesday, March 1, Rubio won his first contest in Minnesota. Cruz won Alaska, Oklahoma and his home state of Texas. Trump won seven states and Ben Carson dropped out of the race a few days later. On March 15, aka Super Tuesday II, Kasich won his first contest carrying his home state of Ohio, but Trump won five states including Florida. Rubio decided to suspend his race since he didn't carry his home state, but retained most of his delegates for the convention.

Now there were only three left, Trump, Cruz and Kasich. In April, Cruz won four western states and Wisconsin, but Trump scored landslide victories in New York and five other North-Eastern states. On May 3, Trump carried every county and every delegate in Indiana, which prevented

Cruz from having any chance for a contested convention. Cruz suspended his campaign and Trump was declared the presumptive nominee by the RNC Chairman. Kasich dropped out the next day.

On May 26, after Washington State voted and a change in delegates in North Dakota was made, the *Associated Press* announced that Trump had secured sufficient votes to place him over the 1,237 delegates needed to secure the nomination. Game over! Or was it? Would the Republican establishment accept Trump as the party's nominee? Would they try to find another candidate to oust Trump at the convention or get some person to run as an alternative to Trump? Would the Libertarian Party find a strong candidate sufficient to threaten Hillary or Trump so that no candidate would get a sufficient number of electors to win and throw the election into the House of Representatives? There are so many issues and so few answers at this time!

My thinking was that we would begin to have a clearer picture within a short time. Political campaigns are so expensive and time consuming that only the most determined will stay in the race until the very end.

The Libertarian Party

On the last weekend in May, 2016, the Libertarian Party met in Orlando, Florida to select their Presidential and Vice-Presidential candidates. After several ballots were cast, the delegates selected Gary Johnson, former Governor of New Mexico as the presidential candidate and William Weld, former Governor of Massachusetts their Vice Presidential candidate.

The party platform opposed taxation in any form and entitlement programs in all forms. They believed federal subsidies to private corporations and all antitrust laws should be eliminated. All government services including the postal service, public schools. Landfills, public property should be transferred to private ownership. They would eliminate antidrug laws, random police roadblocks and legalize prostitution. They would abolish the FCC, the selective service system, and oppose all restrictions on free speech, gun control laws and federal regulations. They promoted pro choice and opposed federal funding of abortions. They believed in open borders so long as these people did not pose a threat to public health or national security. It remained to be seen if this party could acquire sufficient interest to make a difference in this race. Gary Johnson needed to poll at least 15% to be included in the national debates. Would he pose a serious threat to the two main candidates?

I *had serious doubts that this party, with its extreme positions on many issues, would have a major impact on the final outcome of this race. It appeared to be a very close race between Hillary and Trump, but situations can change rapidly in the political world.*

CHAPTER 2

Trump Gets Sidetracked
Late May and June 2016
Trump v. Federal Judge Gonzalo Curiel

Donald Trump decided that Federal Judge Gonzalo Curiel was not being fair to him in the case where several class action plaintiffs had sued Trump University for fraud. Trump went public with his criticism alleging that the judge was hostile toward him and had a bias against him. The judge was of Mexican descent and, therefore, presented a possible conflict of interest because of Trump's prior comments about Mexicans and the country of Mexico. [1]

A judge may not comment or respond to comments such as the ones Trump made. It is against the Code of Judicial Conduct for a judge to make reply to such comments when that judge is involved in an active case.

The news media had a field day commenting on Trump's statement saying the statement was racist. Trump was claiming that Judge Curiel could not do his job because of his race and that he was from Mexico. In fact, the judge was born and raised in Indiana, not Mexico. The press jumped all over these comments, making Trump look biased in the eyes of the American voters. [2]

---

[1] Information furnished by, "*The Indianapolis Star*," in an article by Maureen Groppe dated June 11, 2016.

[2] Information furnished by, "*Milwaukee Journal Sentinel Journal*," by Tom Kertscher dated June 8, 2016. Also information furnished by: CBS News, "Face the Nation," June 5, 2016. CNN, "State of the Union," June 5, 2016. *The Wall Street Journal*, June 3, 2016.

Many Republicans disagreed with Trump, and he finally stopped talking about it. Trump wasted valuable time and got sidetracked from the main issues in this election. CBS News, CNN and *The Wall Street Journal* also carried extensive coverage about Trump's comments. One commentator stated that the American people could care less about this case and its outcome. They wanted to know how Trump was going to solve the many problems that this country was facing. The real question was whether Trump could focus on the main issues and keep from getting sidetracked as he covered the many issues facing the country?

CHAPTER 3

Brexit

The Big Surprise

Trump's Prediction of the Future in the USA

On June 23, 2016, the British people went to the polls to vote on whether the United Kingdom would remain in the European Union (EU) or leave it. The experts, who commented on the outcome, predicted that the voters would strongly favor remaining in the EU. Prior to the election the people betting on the outcome indicated that 75% of those betting favored remaining in the EU, with 25% of the bets placed on leaving. Many of the politicians favored remaining and freely expressed their opinions. Thus, the media formed the opinion that the politicians and those placing their bets knew what the voters would do. The polls closed at 10 p.m. eastern time and the public waited for the favored outcome. However, by early Friday morning the vote tally began to show that the vote was to leave the EU. By 6a.m. Friday morning, the final results revealed that, by a final margin of 52% to 48%, the voters had decided that their country should leave the EU. The voter turnout was extremely high with 72% of the people actually voting. The impact was immediate and severe. At 9:30 a.m. Prime Minister David Cameron announced that he would resign his position to let some other leader guide the country through the withdrawal process. The British pound went down to a 30 year low, the price of gold soared and the U.S. Stock Market reacted by the Dow losing 610 points.

The political impact in the United States was also immediate. Trump congratulated the British voters on regaining their independence and taking control of their borders. He said that the same thing that had taken place in the United Kingdom would also happen in the United States in November when the Presidential election would be held. He said that once again Obama and Hillary got it wrong when they endorsed the idea of the United Kingdom remaining in the EU. He reminded us that the people in the United Kingdom were tired of being ordered around by the people in Belgium and the other countries in the EU and being invaded by foreigners who were taking jobs away from the British people. Just like the politicians in the United States, the British politicians did not understand the feelings of their voters and how angry they were at what had happened to them. Trump just happened to be in Turnberry, Ireland, at the Turnberry Golf Club on Friday morning so he could officially open the club that he had purchased and remodeled. He predicted that he would win the Presidential election because the American people were just as angry as the British.

No one knows the long range impact of this vote. On Monday morning June 27, the U.S. stock market began declining. At 10:30 a.m. the Dow was down almost 300 points and the S&P fell below 2000. At the close on Monday, the Dow was down 260 points to close at 17,140 and the S&P, was down 36 + points to close at 2000. In the last two days two trillion dollars had been lost in the market.

Was Trump correct in saying that this vote was a prediction of the U.S. election in November? Trump seemed to have special insight as to how the people were thinking about many of the issues we faced at this time.

Could it be that Trump was this good at determining the way people will vote in the November election? Just like the British folks, Trump thought the American people were tired of illegal immigrants crossing our Southern border, receiving benefits that they have not earned and taking away jobs that should be filled by Americans.

CHAPTER 4

Radicalized Islamic Terrorism
Goes to Orlando, New York, New Jersey
Then
Global
Gun Control
The Massacre at the Pulse Gay
Night Club in Orlando

Before we begin a discussion of radicalized Islamic terrorism, let me explain why this issue is so important to Americans. Americans want to live in peace and safety, but these ideas are threatened by terrorists, who are in America and all over our globe. We cannot protect ourselves if we have rigid gun control that prevents law abiding citizens from owning a gun. These issues lead to our problems with immigration and our open borders. Congress has refused for years to address our immigration problem. Why? We need immigrants to do the work that Americans won't do, such as in the agriculture industry. Some immigrants take jobs in the tech field because they will work for less pay than the Americans. So here we have many complex issues with few really good answers. We must find answers to immigration, gun control, safety for our citizens, jobs for Americans, law and order, protecting our borders by building walls to keep drugs and illegal immigrants out and building our economy by bringing back jobs lost to other countries because of taxes and cheap labor. We must find a more effective method of vetting immigrants so we can keep the criminals out and those who come here to kill and harm us. These are just a few of the issues that the next president must solve if we are to restore our country to a position of power and respect in the world.

Trump has mentioned on many campaign stops that we are at war with Isis, and we must declare war on them and take all steps necessary to wipe them off the face of the earth. It is his position that they will come to the USA and destroy us if we don't.

On the other hand, Hillary has indicated that we must have strict gun control and find ways to keep terrorists from getting guns, but she has given no details.

We will now examine a series of events that happened in America and worldwide involving terrorism that was believed to be sponsored by radicalized Islamic terrorists.

Orlando

In the early morning hours of June 12, 2016, Omar Mateen entered the Pulse Night Club in Orlando and began to fire a weapon of mass destruction into about 350 people gathered there. He took several patrons hostage, claiming that he was armed with a bomb which he would set off if the police attacked him. For three hours he communicated with various persons by means of a cell phone. Finally, the police decided that he was going to kill many more people if they didn't stop him. They deployed a robot to tear down a wall at the back of the club and enter the club finally locating Omar with the robot killing him.

It was first reported that 20 people had been killed, but this figure was later revised to indicate that Omar had killed 49 people and injured an additional 53 patrons. An investigation revealed that this was the worst mass shooting in the history of the country. The FBI was notified and took over the investigation to determine why Mateen committed this mass murder. It appears Mateen had been investigated by the FBI in the past, but they had insufficient evidence to charge him with a violation of any crime. During the night Mateen made several 911 calls and edited transcripts were released by the FBI and the Department of Justice (DOJ) indicating that the shooting was an act of terror. After many complaints were made to Loretta Lynch, the US Attorney General, she presented an unedited version of the calls showing that Mateen was a Muslim who had been radicalized by Isis and the shooting was confirmed as an act of terror. Mateen had sworn allegiance to Islam, claiming to be an Islamic soldier. It appeared that the DOJ was trying to cover up the fact that Mateen was a radicalized Islamic soldier so as to be politically correct.

Once again, Trump seized upon this opportunity to state that we must find a way to screen these immigrants so that we may determine if they are coming to this country to kill Americans. Trump insisted that we must close our borders to all immigrants who come here to do us harm. He also insisted that we must preserve our right to have guns to protect us from these terrorist acts. He called upon President Obama to finally admit that this was an act of radical Islamic terrorism or resign.

On the other hand, Clinton issued a very different kind of statement urging that we must have strong gun control. She stated that we must find ways to restrict terrorists' access to guns and learn how to deal with such violent acts of terrorism, but gave no details of how this could be accomplished. She offered support for the LGBT community, since the Pulse Nightclub attracted gays, and suggested that we must all stand together as one people and support each other.

Ten days later the House of Representatives held a sit-in to protest the lack of legislation on gun control. Four bills had been introduced, but none passed. Again, the two candidates have different ideas on gun control.

This promises to be one of the key issues to be discussed in the fall. It is my thinking that the American people, now more than ever, do not want controls put on the guns they may own. They believe this will lead to only the criminals and terrorists having guns, and the law abiding people being unable to defend themselves. Hillary is taking a position directly contrary to Trump's idea, and it may come back to haunt her in November.

Terror in NYC Leads to Terror in New Jersey

A Saturday evening explosion that injured 29 people in the Chelsea area of New York City was being investigated as an act of terrorism. A pressure cooker with wires hanging out of it was found nearby and was similar to the one used in the Boston Marathon explosion. The Mayor of

New York indicated this was no accident, but was clearly an intentional act to harm others. One person was in critical condition as a result of the explosion.[3]

Police began a search for the person or persons responsible which led them to New Jersey. The manhunt ended in Linden, New Jersey on Monday when Ahmad Khan Rahami was charged with five counts of attempted murder of a police officer as he was involved in a shootout with police. Ahmad was directly linked to the New York bombing. Further investigation revealed that Ahmad had traveled extensively in the last five years to Afghanistan and Pakistan where he allegedly had family.

The family operates a chicken restaurant in New Jersey and has previously sued the city for discrimination claiming that Linden, New Jersey was harassing them because they were Muslims.[4]

Once again, here we have another example of why the American people seem to be so concerned about these types of events where people are hurt or killed by immigrants conducting acts of terror. The main question is what effect these types of events will have on the election. We were less than two months away from Election Day and Hillary still supported the Obama policies of admitting immigrants to the U. S. On the other hand, Trump indicated that we need to stop admitting immigrants until we have a better system of vetting them.

We are about to find out just how strongly the people feel about what is going on in this country.

It is my thinking that many Americans agree that we should develop a better method of vetting immigrants before admitting them to America. We have many instances where Americans have been hurt or killed by immigrants with ties to Isis. If we are to have a robust economy providing good jobs for our citizens, we must protect our people from jobs being taken by illegal immigrants. On the other hand, we have some jobs, especially in agriculture, where many immigrants are employed because our farmers cannot find citizens willing to work in this area. We have not found a good answer to solve this problem as this issue has not been seriously addressed by either party.

---

[3] Information obtained from CNN by Mallory Simon and Tim Hume dated September 18, 2016.

[4] Information obtained from CNN by Evan Perez and others dated September, 19, 2016.

Hillary agrees with the Obama policy of letting immigrants into the USA even though we do not have an adequate vetting system. Trump opposes Hillary's position.

Turkey

Now we move to Ataturk Airport in Istanbul, Turkey. On June 28, 2016 at approximately 10 PM local time, three terrorists entered the Ataturk Airport, each armed with high-powered assault rifles and began shooting. After the assault ended, 41 people were dead and over 240 injured, six in critical condition. The three terrorist, armed with state of the art bombs, blew themselves up before the end of the attack. All indications point to this attack being well planned and conducted by Isis. This was the fourth and deadliest attack in Istanbul this year. Ataturk is the 11th busiest airport in the world with 61.8 million people traveling through it in 2015.

It is interesting to compare the responses of the two candidates to this event.

Hillary stated this attack strengthens our resolve to defeat the forces of terrorism and radical Jihadist around the world. She continued by saying that the US cannot retreat, and we must deepen our cooperation with our allies and partners in the Middle East and Europe to take on this threat.

Look closely at what she is saying and we conclude that she gives little to no details about how this should be done.

Trump responded that the terrorist threat has never been greater. He stated that our enemies are brutal and ruthless and will do anything to murder those who do not bend to their will. We must take steps now to protect Americans from terrorists and do everything in our power to improve our security to keep America safe. He went on to say that we must fight fire with fire, since Isis cuts off their enemies' heads. Isis also puts their enemies in steel cages, and then drowns them. He believes we must stop being politically correct and learn that Isis will literally do anything to get their way because they perceive us as weak and stupid.

Notice the difference in tone and content between the two statements. Trump gives details and substance to his statements on what must be done to defeat Isis. It will be revealing to see what effect these statements have on the

American voters and if they will influence the outcome of the election in the fall.

I believe fear is a strong motivator. Hillary's comments seem to me to be directed toward our allies instead of Isis. She does not say what we must do to stop Isis from cutting off our heads or what we must do to keep Isis from putting us in steel cages and then drowning us. It looks like political correctness is a weak response to terrorism, and the American people agree with me according to The Washington Post.

Eighty-three per cent of the American voters believed that a terrorist attack in the United States resulting in a large number of casualties is likely in the near future, according to a Washington Post/ABC News poll. A majority believed that our country is at war with "radical Islam." This poll also showed that a majority of Americans wanted the United States to join with our other allies in making a military response to Isis attacks, including increasing air strikes and sending ground troops to fight the Islamic State.[5]

This poll told me that American voters wanted protection from immigrants who would come to America to kill and hurt us. The major question was whether the voters would express this feeling in November?

Global

There seemed to be a pattern forming as Isis continued to spread chaos around the world. Obama said we have Isis contained, but it would appear that this is incorrect. Let's look at a short list of recent events:

November 14, 2015	Paris, France.	killed 137 injured 368
December 9, 2015	San Bernardino, California.	killed 14 injured 22
March 22, 2016	Brussels, Belgium.	32 killed injured 340
June 12, 2016	Orlando, Florida.	killed 49 injured 53
July 1, 2016	Dhaka, Bangladesh.	killed 28 rescued 12
July 4, 2016	Bagdad, Iraq.	Killed 200 injured unknown
July 14, 2016	Bastille Day Paris France	Killed 84 over 200 injured

---

[5] Information furnished by, "*The Washington Post,*" in an article by Scott Clement and Juliet Eilperin dated November 20, 2015.

January 1, 2017   Istanbul, Turkey   Killed 28 injured 239

One of the finest restaurants in downtown Dhaka, known as Holey Artisan Baker, was the scene of another Isis attack on Friday Night, July 1, 2016. After the hostage situation was resolved, 28 people were killed, but 12 were rescued. Isis issued a statement claiming responsibility for the attack. Reports first stated that three Americans were killed, but this figure was not confirmed. Isis also stated attacks in America would be occurring soon. It was July 4th weekend in America, so police were on high alert.

It seemed I couldn't finish writing about one attack until another one appeared. We had just learned that a car bomb exploded in Bagdad, Iraq killing about 200 people with an unknown number injured.

It appeared that these events were helping Trump make his point that we must protect our country. Isis stated that attacks in America were coming soon and I believe this comment concerns all Americans who fear what Isis could do in our country. The people want protection from these radical terrorists and certainly don't want them coming into our country to cut off our heads and drown us. This is a serious threat and it's time to forget about political correctness and take steps to figure out a way to vet all immigrants or prohibit them from coming into our country until we can find a way to make sure they are not coming to kill us.

Bastille Day

It was July 14, 2016, Bastille Day in Nice, France and many families were celebrating on the French Rivera with dinner and fireworks. During the early evening, 31 year old Mohamed Bouhlel drove a large truck into a crowd of celebrating people resulting in the death of 84 people and over 200 injured. Ten of the deceased were children under 10, 50 were in critical condition and 20 were in a coma and on life support. Isis took credit for the attack as it appears that Mohamed was radicalized over the internet in a quick fashion.

Trump postponed his Friday announcement of his VP choice, issuing a statement of sympathy for the families involved and confirming that we are at war with Isis and must stop them from destroying the entire world.

He suggested that the U.S. Congress should issue an official declaration of war against Isis.

Hillary issued a statement of sympathy for the families, confirming that we will not be intimidated. She stated that this only strengthens our commitment to our alliance and defeating terrorism around the world.

So why is this event in France important to the U S and this election? It just so happens that two of the people killed were Americans. A father and son from Austin, Texas were on vacation in Nice with the other members of the family who witnessed this killing. Once again we have Americans being affected by radicalized Islamic terrorism.

I believe this plays right into Trump's plan of declaring war on this group of terrorists and helps his campaign in the eyes of the American voters.

CHAPTER 5

A PRIVATE Meeting Between Bill Clinton and Loretta Lynch

Are You Kidding Me!

Here Comes the FBI

The Wall Street Journal reported in the June 30, 2016 edition that Bill Clinton had a private meeting with Loretta Lynch at the Phoenix, Arizona airport on Tuesday June 28, 2016. Loretta Lynch, as the U.S. Attorney General, would have the final say so on whether Hillary Clinton would be indicted, if the FBI recommended prosecution for violations of various federal laws including the mishandling of top secret and classified information transmitted over an unprotected private server. General Lynch would also have final say on whether Bill Clinton and or Hillary Clinton would be indicted for alleged corruption in their use of Clinton Foundation funds. Where were Ms. Lynch's staff members and Bill's secret service detail during this meeting? Why did someone not advise Bill or Loretta to not have such a meeting because of the appearance of impropriety, even if the investigation was not mentioned or discussed? The status of either of these FBI investigations was not known. Would the FBI recommend prosecution? If they did not, many Americans would conclude one or more of the following conclusions:

1. The judicial system is rigged.
   A. General Lynch blocked the indictment as a favor to Bill and Hillary and in turn Hillary will re-appoint her to another 4 year term if Hillary wins the election.
   B. President Obama ordered General lynch to block the indictment.
   C. The FBI is incompetent.

It was time for the FBI to go public with their findings so that we might know what happened and who did what.

Since Bill Clinton appointed Loretta Lynch to a position of U. S. Attorney when he was president, she owed him a big time favor for promoting her career. *It seemed the better practice would have been to appoint a special prosecutor to handle this entire case so the public would not accuse her of a conflict of interest. How could she be objective in a situation such as this? Bill Clinton and Loretta Lynch were trained in the law and both should have known better than to have a private meeting at a time when Bill and his wife were under federal investigation. Why didn't someone on Loretta's staff advise her not to have the meeting? It is just these types of incidents that destroy the confidence of the American people in our governmental system. Why would either of these legally trained citizens give the people more fuel for saying the "fix" is in and the system is rigged? At the very least this meeting was an exercise in very poor judgment on the part of both parties*

On July 1, 2016, Loretta Lynch announced that she would completely accept the recommendation of the FBI and not substitute her judgment for that of the FBI. Would it be better for her to get out of the case completely and let a special independent prosecutor take over the case?

We had just been told that the FBI would interview Hillary at her house on Saturday, July 2, 2016. Would this lead to her indictment? Would the Democrats draft Vice-President Joe Biden? If they do, would Bernie Sanders and his supporters throw a fit and cause many supporters to vote for Trump? We still had so many questions and so few answers.

From an objective standpoint and based on my prior experience as an Assistant District Attorney General, it still made more sense to me for General Lynch to get out of the case and have some impartial and disinterested person prosecute this case. An independent prosecutor could impanel a Grand Jury, take sworn testimony and see what would develop without concern for the outcome. *This procedure would certainly give the appearance to the American people of a disinterested person in charge of the proceeding with nothing to gain or lose on the outcome. A biased prosecutor is a dangerous thing and can result in an innocent person getting convicted of a crime he or she did not commit. This is one of the greatest concerns of a prosecutor. In the alternative, a biased prosecutor could result in a guilty person being set free on society to continue criminal activity.*

Here Comes the FBI

On Saturday morning, July 2, 2016, (over the July 4th weekend) the FBI spent three and one-half hours questioning Hillary about her use of a private email server and anything else they wanted to know. The interview took place at the FBI headquarters in Washington rather than her home as previously advertised. She was not under oath during the interview, which she voluntarily gave without the necessity of a subpoena. Federal law makes it a crime to lie to the FBI even if she was not under oath. We do not know the results of this event, but it was estimated that they would disclose their findings before the Democratic Convention which would begin July 25, 2016. There was speculation that they would not indict her unless the interview revealed an indictable offense. This meeting took place less than a week after the private meeting between Bill Clinton and Loretta Lynch. Attorney General Loretta Lynch has said that she would follow the recommendation of the FBI and prosecutors in deciding whether to indict Hillary. It was rumored that the FBI was furious that the Attorney General met privately with Bill Clinton, but we have no way to confirm this. General Lynch said that she would not recuse herself from the case, which many took as indicating that she wanted to block any possible indictment of Hillary so Hillary could win the presidency and reappoint Lynch Attorney General for another four year term.

There was a large undercurrent of expectation to know if Hillary would be indicted and all the ramifications of this investigation.

The FBI refused to answer any questions or make any comment about the interview. This is standard operating procedure as the FBI never explains why they do what they do.

The FBI Reports Its Findings

I Don't Get IT

A Double Standard in our Judicial System

On Tuesday, July 5, 2016, FBI Director James Comey reported the findings of the FBI investigation regarding Hillary's email dealings while she was Secretary of State. As a general rule, the FBI never makes a comment or gives an explanation as to why it does not indict the person under investigation. However, in this case Director Comey gave a detailed dissertation on what the FBI found in its investigation and why it did not indict Hillary. The following is a recap of his findings compared to Hillary's public statements on these subject matters.

Hillary: I opted, for convenience sake, to use my personal email account which was allowed.

FBI: SHE WAS EXTREMELY CARELESS IN THE HANDLING OF VERY SENSITIVE AND HIGHLY CLASSIFIED INFORMATION.

Hillary: It was easier for me to carry just one device in the use of my email.

FBI: SHE USED MULTIPLE MOBIL DEVICES TO SEND AND RECEIVE EMAILS.

Hillary: We went through a process to identify all my work related emails and all those emails were delivered to the State Department.

FBI: THE SEARCH FOR EMAILS MISSED SOME WORK RELATED EMAILS AND THERE WAS NO ARCHIVING OR INDEXING OF HER EMAILS.

Hillary: It was my obligation to deliver all my emails to the State Department and I fully fulfilled my obligation.

FBI: HILLARY DELETED ALL HER EMAILS THAT WERE NOT PRODUCED TO THE STATE DEPARTMENT AND HER LAWYERS COMPLETELY CLEARED HER EMAIL SERVER SO AS TO PRECLUDE THE FBI FROM CAPTURING, RETRIEVING OR RECOVERING THE DELETED EMAILS.

Hillary: There were no security breaches.

FBI: IT IS POSSIBLE THAT HOSTILE ACTORS GAINED ACCESS TO HER EMAILS.

Hillary: There was no classified material in the emails.

FBI: ONE HUNDRED AND TEN EMAILS CONTAINED CLASSIFIED MATERIAL AT THE TIME THEY WERE SENT OR RECEIVED. SEVEN OF THESE EMAILS WERE TOP SECRET AT THE TIME THEY WERE SENT OR RECEIVED. THIRTY-SIX EMAILS CONTAINED SECRET INFORMATION AT THE TIME THEY WERE SENT OR RECEIVED. EIGHT OF THESE EMAILS CONTAINED CONFIDENTIAL INFORMATION AT THE TIME THEY WERE SENT OR RECEIVED. SHE SHOULD HAVE KNOWN THAT AN UNCLASSIFIED SYSTEM WAS NO PLACE FOR THESE EMAILS.

Hillary: I was well aware of the classification system for emails and I did not send material marked classified.

FBI: EVEN IF MATERIAL IN EMAILS IS NOT MARKED CLASSIFIED, PARTICIPANTS KNOW OR SHOULD KNOW IF THE SUBJECT MATTER IS CLASSIFIED SO AS TO PROTECT IT.

Hillary: At the time this did not seem like an issue.

FBI: NONE OF THE EMAILS SHOULD HAVE BEEN PRESENT ON AN UNCLASSIFIED SYSTEM.

Summary of the untrue statements told by Hillary:

Her emails contained no classified information.

Her private server was allowed by state Department.

Hillary turned over all work related emails.

She used a single device to send or receive emails.

Her emails were never breached.

The FBI has concluded that Hillary should not be prosecuted for violation of 18USC 793(f) where gross negligence is the standard proof and proof of intent is not necessary. Comey said he could not find a case that would justify prosecution.

Yet, there are many cases where other people have been prosecuted for doing far less. As Rudi Giuliani former US Attorney and Mayor of New York, said, "I am surprised and I profoundly disagree with the position taken by the FBI Director. Only one year ago a Navy engineer, Commander Bryan H. Nishimina, was prosecuted for mishandling classified material when he downloaded classified material onto his personal computer, carried his computer off base and took it home. Then he copied the material onto an unclassified system. He did not distribute or intend to distribute the material. He was prosecuted for a violation of 18USC793 (f). He was fined $7,500.00, placed on 2 years probation and ordered that he never seek or receive clearance to handle classified material. The court specifically found that no intent was necessary for a conviction.

President Obama in April, 2016, said Hillary did not jeopardize U. S. national security at a time when the FBI was still investigating her. This statement is contrary to the FBI findings later released to the public. He gave no explanation for his conclusion.

It was just eight days before Comey's announcement that Bill Clinton met privately with Loretta Lynch on the tarmac of the Phoenix, Arizona airport. *The New York Times* reported that Bill Clinton offered to keep Loretta on as Attorney General in the Clinton administration if she did not indict Hillary. On its face this appeared to be a deal where Loretta Lynch blocked the indictment in return for an appointment by Hillary as Attorney General for four more years.

The American people do not understand what is going on. They are thinking that the government is corrupt and this election is rigged. They feel that Hillary and Bill Clinton are above the law. There seems to be no consequences or accountability for the many untruths Hillary has told. Why has Hillary not lost her security clearance after being "extremely careless" with the use of her emails? It looks like she had 30,000 emails destroyed. They cannot be recreated or retrieved. As Rep. Bob Goodlatee said, "This stinks."

A *Washington Post* poll revealed that 58% of the people disagreed with the FBI report compared to 35% who agree. It appeared to the American people that there was a double standard of justice- one standard of overlooking for the rich and famous and another more severe standard for the ordinary person.

Chuck Todd felt that the FBI had indicted her politically as they have proven that she has very poor judgment, is unqualified to hold national security secrets, and that she simply cannot be trusted.[6]

Was it possible that Director Comey was blocked from indicting Hillary? Did he decide to disclose the finding of his investigation so the American people could know what happened and not vote for Hillary?

---

[6] Information furnished by "*Townhall,*" in article by Matt Vespa on July 7, 2016.

It appeared that the FBI had just given the GOP an issue which might push Hillary into a loss in the fall election.

In my opinion, you could bet that Trump would use this information to reinforce the idea of Hillary as "Crooked Hillary," a term he repeated often during his speeches.

We now have a case where Kristian Saucier, a 22 year old U S Navy machinist mate, took six photos inside the USS Alexandria nuclear submarine with the photos classified as "confidential," the lowest level of classification. He took the photos so he could show them to his future children. His attorney argued that he should receive probation since his photos were of a much lower classification than Hillary's. Three of Hillary's emails were classified as "Top Secret." The sailor received a sentence of one year in prison, a $100 fine, six months home confinement, 100 hours of community service and a ban on owning any guns. Hillary wasn't even charged. So if your last name is Clinton you go free, but if your last name is Saucier you go to prison.

Many voters point to this case to support the idea that we do in fact have a double standard when deciding who should be punished for mishandling classified information.

If Director Comey was blocked from recommending that Hillary be indicted, then he used a very effective news conference to tell in detail what Hillary had done and, in effect, indicted her politically.

There appears to be a growing anger and disappointment toward Hillary after Comey's report.

If Comey did politically indict Hillary, will the American people find her guilty by electing Trump?

CHAPTER 6

The Polls and Hillary's Email Scandal

July 4, 2016

Several recent polls were showing this to be a crazy election. The *NBC/WSJ* poll had Hillary leading 46% to 41%, a 5 point lead. *The ABC/Washington Post* poll reflected Hillary 51% to 39%, a 12 point difference. A *Quinnipiac University* polls showed Trump 44% to Hillary 41%, a 3 point lead for Trump. Nate Silver said Hillary had a 79% chance of winning the election, and he had a reputation of being accurate most of the time. So which poll was more accurate? What was going on and why was there such a drastic difference in the various polls?

It could be that the difference in the polls was due to the size of the sample conducted or that the sample was not a truly random survey of the entire population. Thus, the poll takers may be consulting more Democrats than Republicans or vice versa without realizing it, or could it be on purpose? Some voters believed the media was showing Hillary with a lead because they wanted her to win. We would only know for sure after the election was over as to who was the most accurate. It appeared that Hillary had a lead of 5 to 10 points, but the latest polls showed Trump closing on Hillary's lead of 1 to 2 points as of July 4, 2016. The one thing we knew for sure was that the poll taken was only an estimate of the results at the exact time it was taken. Things could change often until the election was held.

There is another angle to all these polls. Some political analysts thought the people were hiding their true opinions about who they favored because they did not want anyone to know how they really felt. There was an amazing amount of distrust by the people toward the candidates and toward the government.

I talked to several people about who they favored and most of them quietly whispered to me that I can't tell anyone what they say and then they said they are going to vote for Trump. They go on to say that they have concerns about Trump, but that they don't like Hillary, her dishonesty and carelessness when dealing with classified information as Secretary of State. They also don't believe the polls because the polls are controlled by biased people. My conclusion is that the people don't trust the politicians, the candidates, the media, the polls, the establishment and big government. So it appears that the best rule is to not put much faith in the polls.

The Email Scandal Continues

July 5, 2016

During the Congressional Benghazi hearing on October 22, 2015, when Hillary was under oath, she testified that she never sent emails that were marked "classified." When FBI Director James Comey was asked on July 5, 2016, if that statement was true, he stated that this statement was not true as Hillary did in fact send 110 emails that were marked as "classified."

When Comey was asked if this constituted perjury, he said yes. He was asked why he did not recommend indictment on this information. He replied that it was not within the scope of his investigation. He further said that he had not received a written request from Congress to investigate this matter, but upon receipt of such a request, the FBI would investigate.

It seems that the email problem has not disappeared. The chairman of the Congressional Benghazi Committee implied that a letter would be forthcoming to the FBI requesting that it investigate perjury charges against Hillary as a result of Comey statements.

It appeared to me that almost every day there was some event that put one or both of these candidates in more trouble than they were in the day before the event. Here we appear to have a certain case of perjury against Hillary. The more she does the more the trouble mounts as it is uncovered. Perjury is a felony and is not to be taken lightly. Would the voters elect a candidate suspected of a sure case of perjury? If Obama were to pardon her, would the voters still vote for her? It seemed to be a never ending saga of trouble for her as the race continued to November

CHAPTER 7

Dump Trump?
The Hot Summer of 2016
"I'm Mad as Hell and
I'm Not Going to Take It Anymore"

This famous quote from the movie, *"Network,"* pretty well describes the feelings of the American voters and the Washington power brokers in the summer of 2016. The people have decided to vote for Trump and make him the presumptive Republican nominee. Trump got more votes in the primaries than any other candidate in the history of the GOP Party. Wouldn't you think they would be celebrating? Yet, three weeks away from the GOP convention they still weren't happy. The Republican establishment, Washington power brokers and lobbyists were upset at the voters for selecting Trump as their nominee and were still trying to figure out a way to get rid of him. Many of the elected Republican politicians were refusing to appear at the convention. The Washington power people were angry because they were losing control over the nominee and, therefore, losing power over the country. Trump couldn't be bought and refused to cow to their every wish. The lobbyists are furious because Trump wouldn't take their money which meant he wouldn't take their advice.

As of 2014, there were estimated to be about 12,281 registered lobbyists in Washington, but many of them have gone underground resulting in a more accurate estimate of about 100,000 lobbyists who spend an estimated $9 billion per year.[7]

How scary is this information? Very! That amounts to $900 million per lobbyist which will buy a lot of influence. Now you know why it is said that we have the finest politicians money can buy. No one knows how much the power brokers want to keep control.

The politicians are irate because they are being told to be this way. The power brokers have lots of other candidates to choose from even if the Republican voters did not vote for them. The real issue is whether these power people have the guts to overthrow the people's wishes, nominate some other candidate, run off the GOP voters and risk losing the election to Hillary.

The voters are peeved to put it mildly. They are tired of do-nothing politicians. The politicians get elected and immediately start to raise money for their next election. The problem is it costs too much money to run a campaign. Many promote campaign finance reform so the politicians can spend time solving the people's problems and focus on the issues they face in running government effectively, rather than raising money for their next campaign. The present system leads to electing the politicians who are obligated to their contributors rather than electing the finest politicians to govern our country.

Yet, when finance reform was discussed it seemed to get nowhere. The lobbyists and power brokers don't want finance reform. They want power and control over the politicians. The main question was whether the people will refuse to listen to the news press, TV stations, lobbyists, Washington establishment, bought politicians and wealthy contributors and elect a rebel like Trump? Who said democracy wasn't interesting?

Is anybody happy with the state of affairs? Yes, the Democrats were thrilled because they saw an opposition party in shambles. Hillary's most wonderful dream is coming true. When the Republicans nominated Trump, did she think she could gallop right into the White House on her beautiful white horse?

What is the answer to this mess? I believe we must figure out a way to enact term limits for all those who serve in elected positions in Washington. The President has term limits of two four year terms, but the Senators and Congressmen have no limitation on how many terms they may serve. All serving in The House of Representatives must run for re-election every two

---

[7] Data taken from *Wikipedia:"Lobbying in the United States."*

years, while Senators must run for re-election every six years. If we enact term limits, maybe those serving can focus on solving our problems rather than raising money for re-election. Changing term limits may be easier said than done as it takes a change in the constitution.

Article Five of the U.S. Constitution governs changes to be made which are done by an amendment. The amendments may be proposed either by Congress with a two-thirds vote in both the House of Representatives and the Senate or by a convention of the states called for by two-thirds of the state legislatures. To become a part of the constitution, an amendment must be ratified by either the legislatures of three-quarters of the states or state ratifying conventions in three-quarters of the states. [8]

I think term limits for Congress is way overdue, but I think it is going to take a lot of pressure from the people to get it done. I don't see Congress being willing to limit terms of office so the people will have to put pressure on the state legislatures to demand a change in term limits.

Just how upset must the people get before they insist on term limits?

---

[8] Information obtained from *Wikipedia* in an article entitled, *"Article Five of the United States Constitution."*

CHAPTER 8

Trump's Vice President

Who will Trump pick for his vice president? It's July 4, 2016, only 13 days until the start of the GOP convention so let's take a look at the possible candidates:

- Newt Gingrich: a former Speaker of the House and a very experienced politician. Trump can use a person with wisdom in this area, but he is 73 and comes with some serious baggage in his personal life, which may keep him from getting this position.
- Bob Corker: a Senator from Tennessee and chairman of the Senate Foreign Relations Committee, so he could be a great help to Trump. He is cool, calm and collected, plus an excellent speaker. He would help Trump in the South, but Trump needs his wisdom in foreign affairs so he may be more help to Trump if he remains in the Senate.
- Jeff Sessions: a Senator from Alabama. He has lots of experience in the Senate and makes a good impression, but like Corker, it may be more valuable to Trump for him to remain in the Senate or become a member of the cabinet. He is a former U.S. Attorney from Alabama and was denied Senate approval when he was nominated to become a U.S. Federal Judge.
- Paul LaPage: Governor of Maine and an early supporter, but does not have much of a chance.
- Chris Christe: Governor of New Jersey. He is a fire ball, but appears to be a better choice for Attorney General. He is a former U.S. Attorney with prosecution experience. He is currently helping

Trump with a transition team assuming Trump wins, but he also has a lot of serious personal problems, which hurt his chances.

- Scott Brown: a former Senator but does not have much of a chance.
- Mike Huckabee: a former governor of Arkansas and an excellent speaker, but not much of a chance.
- John Kasich: the Governor of Ohio. He is not very dynamic, but is well liked and respected. Trump needs to carry Ohio to win, but he has not supported Trump so he does not have much of a chance.
- Rick Scott: the Governor of Florida. He is not well liked, but Trump needs Florida to win the presidency. He also has a lot of serious baggage which may hurt his chances.
- Mike Pence: the Governor of Indiana and is a 12 year veteran of the U.S. House of Representatives. He has lots of political experience, and is a religious and political conservative, who has close ties to Paul Ryan, the current Speaker of the House. He just may be Trump's best choice.
- Sarah Palin: a former Governor of Alaska and VP running mate with John McCain. She does not have much of a chance as many believe she hurt McCain in the last election.
- Joni Ernst: a Senator from Iowa and is a conservative who is well respected and who could help Trump with the women voters. Trump needs a lot of help in this area.

My guess was that it would be either Corker or Pence. Both are experienced, conservative and good speakers.

This may be the most important decision Trump must make if he is to win in November!

It's Vice-President Selection Time

On Wednesday, July 13, 2016, all the experts believed it was down to four candidates: Gov. Mike Pence of Indiana; Gov. Chris Christie of New Jersey; Senator Jeff Sessions of Alabama and former Speaker of the House Newt Gingrich. Rumors were that Trump favors Christie, while Trump's children favor Pence. Many thought Senator Sessions was out and would be of more benefit to Trump by staying in the Senate or filling some cabinet position. That leaves Speaker Gingrich, who many thought might already have the job with Trump trying to keep the TV stations busy with free publicity. Pence must tell his state by Friday if he is going to run for Vice President. He cannot run for governor and Vice-President at the same time and so he must withdraw his name from consideration at that time. My guess was that Trump would wait to the last minute to announce his choice, again to create interest and free advertising in his selection. Trump must leave for California to appear at a fundraiser Thursday so he asked his children to finish the interview process. Trump would return to announce his decision on Friday. Trump listened to his children, so it may be Pence.

On Wednesday, July 13, 2016, many of the news channels continued to report on who Trump might select. Once again, Trump figured out how to dominate the coverage on most of the news channels. He got many dollars worth of free advertising just by staging the announcement of his V.P. choice.

On Thursday afternoon about 1 *p.m.* Bloomberg News Channel flashed a special message that Pence was Trump's choice to fill the V.P. slot. They indicated that they had not been able to confirm this information, but would keep us posted. A few minutes later, CNN reported that Pence was believed to be the choice. They were also trying to receive confirmation of this report. They announced that the official announcement would be made by Trump at 11 *a.m.* on Friday in New York. So here we go again with all the major TV channels on Thursday afternoon covering the possible selection of Gov. Pence as the V.P. For two days in a row, Trump has taken over the news of all the major news stations. He appeared to be a master at obtaining free publicity about what his campaign is doing.

I went to my computer, turned on MSN.com and up flashed, "Ten things we should know about Mike Pence, Trump's likely running mate." The program indicated that he grew up as a Democrat, but now was the 57 year old Republican Governor of Indiana. He spent six terms (12 years) in Congress, was a social conservative and devout Christian who would shore up support among the evangelicals. Many of them are weary of Trump. Pence first endorsed Ted Cruz, then Trump, and he was an advocate for the Tea Party movement. He and Paul Ryan are personal friends, and he has ties to the Koch brothers. It appears that Trump's children won the battle.

My thinking is that Pence is an excellent choice for a win. He has 12 years experience in the House and is the current Governor of Indiana. He has the political experience and relationships that Trump does not have as he is known to be a conservative, friendly and, approachable with a good relationship with many in Congress. Just think, if Trump wins, this will be his first political victory, as he has no experience as a politician. This is why Pence will be of great benefit to Trump. These two men are different in many ways, but each fills in gaps that the other person has so they complement each other very well. This just may turn out to be a winning ticket.

It's Official

Mike Pence is selected as Vice President Candidate

On Saturday morning July 16, 2016 at 11a.*m.* Trump made it official by selecting Gov. Mike Pence of Indiana as his running mate. He pointed out the outstanding accomplishments of Gov. Pence in cutting taxes in Indiana while increasing jobs. He also confirmed that more money had been spent on improving education in Indiana. Governor Pence was a 12 year member of Congress serving as a Republican Party leader for part of this time. He has been Governor of Indiana since 2013.

So the question must be asked as to why Trump did not select some of the other persons mentioned for consideration. Let's go down the list.

Dr. Ben Carson was an early supporter once he dropped out of the race. Would he be better suited as Surgeon General, Secretary of Health or some other cabinet position?

Chris Christie, one time Trump's favorite, was not selected because he was too much of an attack dog like Trump and Trump's children preferred Pence. Many thought Christie would be our next U S Attorney General, replacing Loretta Lynch. He is a former U S Attorney so he has experience in this position and will be an effective administrator and prosecutor. His prior legal problems could affect his appointment as it appears he has some problems to resolve in New Jersey.

Newt Gingrich was considered the first choice at one time and came close to being selected, but he was 73 years old and brought a lot of baggage with him. Many felt he would end up as Chief of Staff or possibly even Secretary of State. He was a former Speaker of the House and had a ton of experience in dealing with Congress. He could also be of help in dealing with foreign countries. His problem was that he also had some baggage in his past that might even keep him from getting any position in a Trump administration.

Bob Corker, Senator from Tennessee, is chairman of the Senate Foreign Relations Committee and at one time was under serious consideration. He may be more valuable to Trump in his present position, but he could be under consideration as Secretary of State.

Senator Jeff Sessions of Alabama was also considered, but he was a 19 year member of the Senate and had served on many committees. He may be more valuable to Trump in the Senate or in a cabinet position.

Another Republican who bears mention is Herman Cain, a retired pizza executive who ran for President 4 years ago. A gifted speaker with a lot of common sense, this African-American Republican would be put to good use in attracting his race to vote for Trump.

It appeared there is a lot of talent on the Republican side and not much talent on the Democratic side. I could be wrong, but this is the way it seems to me.

CHAPTER 9

Police and Race Relations in the USA

Dallas, Texas

On Tuesday morning, July 5, 2016, Alton Sterling, an African-American motorist, was shot and killed by a white police officer in Baton Rouge, La. The next day, Philando Castile, an African-American motorist, was shot and killed by a white police officer in St. Paul, Minnesota. Both of these incidents were the result of a simple traffic stop. This led to a peaceful Black Lives Matter demonstration in Dallas, Texas that turned violent on July 7, 2016, when Micha Johnson, an Army veteran who was also believed to be associated with the Black Panthers or Black Power Groups, started shooting his semi-automatic rifle at white police officers. He said he wanted to kill white people, but especially wanted to kill white police officers. Johnson shot and killed 5 Dallas officers and wounded 7 others. He refused to surrender after being cornered in a parking lot. He wore ballistic body armor with plates and had two hand guns on him besides the rifle. Finally, a bomb-loaded robot was used to kill Johnson. An investigation into this killing revealed that Johnson was an Afghanistan veteran having symptoms of PTSD, aka Post Traumatic Stress Disorder.

Trump and Clinton cancelled campaign appearances and each issued statements of sympathy for all persons involved. Trump went on to say that we must restore law and order so that our citizens will have confidence to be safe and secure in their homes and on the streets of our cities. Hillary indicated that she mourned for the lives lost and spoke with the Dallas Mayor to offer any assistance she could provide.

How will each candidate deal with the problem of race relations and the police as the fall campaign proceeds?

This may be one of the more difficult issues facing the candidates.

The Violence against Police Officers Spreads to Baton Rouge La

Three policemen killed Sunday Morning July 17, 2016

Three police officers were killed Sunday morning and another three were wounded by an African-American who was a former marine. He was believed to be upset at police shootings of blacks and came from Missouri to kill police officers. Baton Rouge Officers killed the attacker, 29 year old Gavin Lang, during the shooting spree. No motive was given for the attack other than the hatred of the police. This supports the theory of Trump that our country is in chaos over police officers shooting blacks and, in turn, blacks seeking revenge against white police officers.

We need to appoint a special prosecutor to investigate what is causing so many police officers to shoot blacks and what can be done to restore order to our country. Police officers are sworn to protect us and keep us safe and secure from harm. Many officers put their lives on the line every day to see this idea carried out. If the officers are not doing their duty, they need to be fired. If they are breaking the law, they need to be prosecuted. Likewise, if the violent blacks are violating the law, they need to be prosecuted and stop taking the law into their own hands. We need an exhaustive investigation into this issue so we can understand how to better deal with these issues.

Until we have all the facts surrounding the causes of this type of conduct on the part of the police and the African-American, we will not know what course of action to take to remedy the situation. One thing is very clear. We need this situation corrected and stopped so that all Americans, regardless of gender or color, can live in a peaceful and safe environment where justice and fairness prevail. Until we have this investigation conducted by an independent prosecutor, we may continue to have this type of violent behavior. I believe the independent prosecutor should be neither black nor white, but from a different race. This will help the public have more confidence in the results of the investigation.

On April 8, 2017 the Fox Business News Network presented a program by John Stossel revealing that an investigation in Orlando, Florida showed that police officers wearing cameras was leading to a 65% reduction of complaints against police officers. It is interesting to note that ongoing required training for police officers was leading to a reduction of police over-aggression.

These are just two ideas that might help to improve this situation. What will the next president promote for improvement in this area?

CHAPTER 10

U. S. Supreme Court Justice
Ruth Bader Ginsberg
She Said What?

The eighty-three year old liberal Supreme Court Justice Ruth Bader Ginsberg has publically indicated that Trump should not be elected President as he is inconsistent, has a large ego, is a faker and should show his tax returns to the public. She also indicated that if he wins, it's time to move out of the country because he would be a dangerous president.

Justice Ginsberg was trying to influence the outcome of the nomination process by suggesting that Trump was not presidential material. Since she is a liberal Democrat, I doubt that she will have much influence on the delegates to the GOP convention, which starts in just a few days. As the oldest member of the court, I believe it's time for her to consider retirement

Legal ethical scholars commented that it was not proper for a Supreme Court Justice to comment on candidates in an election. It put her in a position of having to recuse herself from deciding any case in which Trump is a party as an individual or as president. With the court having only 8 members at this time, it is even more important that she should not have made any public statement regarding his fitness to serve as president.

Trump countered that her comments were not appropriate for a justice of the Supreme Court and she should apologize for her statements. Trump went on to imply that she has problems with her mind and should get off the court soon. It is not clear what effect her comments will have on the voters.

Several days later, Justice Ginsberg apologized for her comments and promised to be more careful in the future.

People need to understand that when you attack Trump, he is going to respond by fighting back. So be careful what you say and be prepared to face the consequences if you are willing to take Trump on!

CHAPTER 11

The Polls before the Conventions

July 13, 2016

It was just 5 days before the start of the GOP convention and the new polls revealed some interesting data. The Quinnipiac University poll for Florida showed:

Trump 42

Clinton 39

This is a loss of 11 points for Clinton in one month.

For Pennsylvania:

Trump 43

Clinton 41

A three point loss for Clinton in one month.

For Ohio:

Trump 41

Clinton 41

The polls also show that the people think Trump is more honest and trustworthy than Clinton.

The Monmouth University Poll shows:

For Iowa:

Trump 44

Clinton 42

Johnson 6 The Libertarian Party

The poll taken for voters under age 50 revealed:

Trump 51

Clinton 32

Johnson 7

Trump has a 19 point lead in this age group.

The Harper poll shows

For Colorado:

Clinton 45

Trump 38

Others 14

These polls show Trump with momentum going into the GOP convention which may help unify the party and discourage anyone from trying to dump Trump. Were these polls showing a positive move for Trump or were they revealing a negative trend against Hillary? If we look at Florida, it would appear that Hillary had lost 11 points in just one month indicating that there was a trend beginning to appear that voters were distrusting, "Crooked Hillary," and starting to think Trump might "Make America Great Again." One of the above polls supports this idea in that the people think Trump is more honest and trustworthy. Will the powerbrokers still try to dump Trump in favor of some other candidate they can control?

It is interesting to see that Trump is gaining in Pennsylvania, Ohio and Iowa. Trump needs Florida and these three other states if he is going to win.

History tells us that the nominee will get a boost coming out of the convention. It could be an exciting week ahead for the GOP.

How much could we trust these polls? They seemed to be all over the board which would lead one to disbelieve their results. So much depends on who is conducting the polls and how honest they are in picking their sample. Are they actually picking a random sample? Do they have a hidden motive?

We have so many questions with so few answers.

CHAPTER 12

The Political Parties Hold their Conventions

The Nomination Process Completed

The Candidates Selected

Welcome to Cleveland, Ohio

The GOP Convention

July 18-July 21, 2016

Will the GOP Delegates Dump Trump?

The GOP Convention began with an attempt to dump Trump. The Rules Committee stopped this attempt in haste, so the anti-Trump protesters began to voice their displeasure by forming outside the convention where they made a lot of noise, but without results.

The theme of each night was:

Monday: Make American Safe Again

Tuesday: Make America First Again

Wednesday: Make America Work Again

Thursday: Make America One Again

The balance of the convention went as planned with the exception of Ted Cruz who refused to endorse Trump and was booed off the stage at the end of his speech. Mike Pence gave his acceptance speech as vice president. He was very supportive of Trump.

The last night, Trump was introduced by his oldest daughter, Ivanka Trump, who appeared poised and at ease as she talked warmly about her father and his accomplishments.

The highlight of the evening was Trump's acceptance speech as the party's nominee for president. He gave a lengthy talk about his plan for the country and was well received by the delegates. The public had been led to believe that the GOP Convention would be full of chaos and trouble for Trump, but it turned out to be supportive and celebratory compared to the Democratic Convention which followed the next week.

It appeared to me that the delegates to the GOP Convention were dedicated to a Trump nomination and nothing was going to stop them from voting for him. My thinking was that many voters in America felt the exact same way and were quietly waiting for Election Day to express their preference for a change and vote for Trump.

Trump continued to place an emphasis on his rallies which were drawing huge crowds. Television stations cover many of them which gives him free press coverage and advertising for him to talk about:

- Building a wall on our southern border.
- Protecting our country from immigrants who come here to harm us.
- Repealing and replacing Obamacare.
- Creating good-paying jobs for American workers.
- Lowering our personal and corporate taxes.
- Putting America first.
- Making America safe again
- Restoring law and order to our communities.
- Giving parents child care benefits to assist them in their work.
- Wiping Isis off the face of the earth.
- Stopping terrorists from destroying our way of life in America.
- Placing term limits on all members of Congress.
- Removing America from NAFTA
- Placing limits on lobbyists.

- This information furnished by CNN
- Removing America from the Trans-Pacific Partnership

The people seemed to love his ideas. Trump appeared to love being among the people. The crowds seemed to get bigger as time for the election neared. Trump focused on hot-button issues which have been festering underground for years, so a ground swell of voters may be motivated to go to the polls. For example, the voters were tired of seeing illegal immigrants and drugs pour across our southern border, which were two problems which were present for many years. Would these issues translate into votes on Election Day, especially since Trump rallies always get the people to say, "Build the wall?"

Welcome to Philadelphia, Pa.

The Democratic Convention

July 25- July 28, 2016

Pre-Convention activity

Tim Kaine, Hillary's V.P. Choice

WikiLeaks Appears on the Scene

On Saturday, July 23, 2016, Hillary held a rally in Miami at which she introduced Tim Kaine as her VP choice. Kaine, a moderate senator from Virginia, with lots of political experience including being a former Mayor of Richmond, former Governor of Virginia and a former chairman of the Democratic National Convention. Bernie Sander's delegates were upset that she did not pick Bernie, a liberal, to be V.P. as she decided on a more moderate choice.

On Sunday, July 24, 2016, it was revealed that WikiLeaks had hacked several thousand emails belonging to the Democratic National Committee. This showed that the committee had taken action to favor the nomination of Hillary Clinton over Bernie Sanders, thereby taking control of the outcome of the primaries rather than letting the people decide who should get the nomination. The committee was established to be impartial in governing the primary process, but the process was "rigged" by the members. Bernie Sanders' delegates immediately began to protest on Sunday afternoon before the convention was to start on Monday. They made signs saying "Rigged," and "Hillary Lies and is Evil." It was announced that Debbie Wasserman Schultz, the convention chairman, would open and close the convention. She would not speak at the convention and would resign immediately following the convention. Monday morning Debbie addressed the Florida delegation, but was booed off the platform and it was decided that she would immediately be removed from any part in the convention. A temporary chair, Marcia Fudge, was selected who was an unknown congresswoman.

Bernie Sanders was to speak on Monday evening and many delegates expected him to question the outcome of the rigged primaries, but he did not and the delegates were upset. When he endorsed Hillary and requested his delegates to support her, his delegates booed him and this only angered the delegates more that the "Fix" was in for Hillary. It appeared that he did not really want the nomination or he would have said more about the corruption of the election process. It was announced that Hillary had appointed Debbie Wasserman Schultz as The Honorary National Chairwoman of her campaign, which Bernie's delegates interpreted as a payoff for rigging the primaries in Hillary's favor.

Wednesday, Tim Kaine addressed the convention and on Thursday Chelsea Clinton introduced her mother who accepted the democratic nomination for president.

All of these talks were overshadowed by the father of a deceased Muslim U.S. soldier who spoke about his son's sacrifice for our country. He was killed in Iraq by a bomb. Khizr Khan, with his wife at his side, talked about their son, Humayun, who was a Captain in the U.S. Army and awarded a Purple Heart and Bronze Star posthumously. He said "we are patriotic American Muslims with undivided loyalty to our country." He went on to say, "Our son gave up his dream to become a military lawyer so he could join the fight on the front lines of the battle." Then he turned his attention toward Donald Trump saying, "If it was up to Donald Trump, Humayun would have never been in America…He smears the character of Muslims…disrespects other minorities, women, judges, even his own party leadership. He vows to build walls and ban us from this country". He went on to talk about the U.S. Constitution,

---

mentioning liberty and equal protection of the law. He invited Trump to visit Arlington Cemetery where you will see the graves of brave patriots who died defending America. You will see all faiths, genders and ethnicities. He closed by saying Trump had sacrificed nothing and no one. This speech hit the airwaves and social media with great impact. Gold star mothers were mad that Trump showed such little respect for Ms. Kahn when he criticized her for not saying anything during the speech. Hillary jumped on this comment and a lot of women were turned off by Trump's comments. The news media ran a video of the father's speech and, as late as August 18, we were able to go on the internet to find a video of the speech and an interesting article by Doug Mastaconis an attorney who writes for *"Outside the Beltway."* Trump will have a hard time living down his reaction to the speech by Mr. Kahn, and he had to hear a lot of negative response from the media about this.

In fact, the post Democratic convention polls showed that Hillary got a substantial boost in the national polls and many attribute some of this increase to the speech by Mr. Kahn. Hillary got a national lead of 6 to 9 points, whereas before the convention, Trump had a national lead by approximately 4 points. After the convention, Hillary maintained her lead and in some cases increased it to the extent that Trump was now losing in some key states such as Florida, Pennsylvania, Ohio and Virginia. He must win these states if he planned on winning the election. He must have a change in strategy if he was to reverse this trend. Hillary now led Trump 42 to 34 in the latest national poll. Another 23% said they would not vote for either candidate. Hillary's support ranged from 44% to 41 % while Trump's support ranged from 33% to 39%. Neither candidate was viewed favorably due to all the negative press about both candidates. The polls also showed 2/3 of the voters saying the country is on the wrong track.

If there was no change in Trump's planning, I believed Trump would lose the election due to the current trend that seemed to favor Hillary. The closer we got to Election Day, the harder it would be for Trump to overcome Hillary's lead.

Would Trump make the necessary changes in his campaign to improve his chances of winning? Donald Trump had a lifetime of successful business ventures, much of which was in the public arena. He had many admirers.

Hillary Clinton was an admirable woman in many respects; she had a public service record covering her lifetime of service as a lawyer, governor's wife, president's wife, senator, and Secretary of State.

The Political Parties Complete the Nomination Process

Hillary Clinton, the Democratic Nominee for President

and

Donald Trump, the Republican Nominee for President

The Main Characters in this Book

Hillary Diane Rodham Clinton was born October 26, 1947 in Chicago, Illinois and raised in the Chicago suburb of Park Ridge. Her father, Hugh, was manager of a small but successful textile business. Her mother, Dorothy Howell, was a homemaker. Hillary has two younger brothers, Hugh and Tony. In high school she participated in the student council, the school newspaper, the National Honor Society, became a National Merit Finalist and was voted "most likely to succeed." She was raised in a politically conservative home and took part in various Republican activities during her high school and college years.

She attended Wellesley College where she was elected president of the Wellesley College Government Association and became the first student in the history of the college to speak at her commencement. She graduated with a Bachelor of Arts degree and received departmental honors in political science.

After graduation from Wellesley, she enrolled in Yale Law School where she served on the editorial board of the Law Review and Social Action. While attending law school she worked at the Yale Child Study Center doing research on early childhood brain development and was involved in various political activities including assisting Democratic candidate George McGovern in his unsuccessful bid to become president. She dated Bill Clinton during her law school years, but declined his proposal for marriage at that time. After graduation she assisted the House Judiciary Committee on the Watergate scandal by doing research on impeachment procedures regarding Richard Nixon, who later resigned. Hillary enrolled in a postgraduate study on children at the Yale Child Study Center while Bill Clinton continued to make proposals for marriage.

After failing the District of Columbia bar exam and passing the Arkansas bar exam, she moved to Arkansas, married Bill Clinton and began teaching criminal law at the School of Law at the University of Arkansas. She joined the Rose Law Firm, a famous law firm with substantial political and economic influence in Arkansas. Bill ran successfully for Attorney General and later Governor of Arkansas. In 1980, Hillary gave birth to a daughter, Chelsea. After his service as Governor Bill Clinton ran a successful campaign for president and Hillary became First Lady. [9] She later was elected as a U.S. Senator for New York. Hillary ran for president seeking the Democratic nomination, but lost her bid to Barack Obama, who later appointed her Secretary of State of the United States. It was during her tenure as Secretary of State in December 2011 that Hillary made the statement that Russia's election of Putin was "dishonest and unfair, which produced widespread allegations of fraud and vote-rigging and angered Putin greatly." When protestors accused Putin of having rigged the recent election, he blamed Hillary, claiming she was trying to undermine his power. She stated further that "the Russian people deserve to have their voices heard and their votes counted, and that means they deserve fair, free transparent elections and leaders who are accountable to them."[10]

In March of 2014 Hillary, commenting on Russia's annexation of Crimea, said that Putin's actions were like "what Hitler did back in the 1930's." Her statements about Putin add insight into why Putin greatly disliked Hillary, and why she became the target of Putin's aggression. Her comments about Putin help explain why he took action to see that Hillary was defeated in this race, and why Putin may have directed the email hack of the Democratic National Committee.

---

[9] Information obtained from *Wikipedia*

[10] *Politico Magazine*, in an article dated July 25, 2016 titled: "Why Putin Hates Hillary," by Michael Crowley and Julia Offe.

The Trump Family

Donald Trump was born June 14, 1946, in New York City where he lived until age 13, when he enrolled in New York Military Academy. He received an economics degree from The Wharton School of the University of Pennsylvania in 1968. In 1971 he took charge of the family real estate and construction firm which became The Trump Organization. Trump built, renovated and managed numerous office towers, hotels, casinos and golf courses. He formerly owned the Miss USA and Miss Universe pageants. He hosted "The Apprentice," a TV show until he resigned to run for president.

In 2000 he sought The Reform Party presidential nomination but withdrew prior to the beginning of the voting. In 2015 he announced his candidacy for president by seeking the Republican Party nomination and running against 17 other candidates. In July 2016, he secured the presidential nomination and ran against Hillary Clinton.

In November 2016 he defeated Hillary Clinton in a surprise victory and became the oldest and wealthiest person to become President of the United States without prior military or government service. He became the fifth person elected without carrying the popular vote. He has five children and eight grandchildren.

Our First Lady, Melania Trump was born April 20, 1970, in Solvenia, Yugoslavia. She became an American citizen on 2006 and worked as a model until her marriage to Donald Trump in 2005. On March 20, 2006 she gave birth to Barron Trump, their only child. Trump has three children by his first wife, Ivana. They are Donald Trump, Jr., Eric and Ivanka Trump. He has a daughter, Tiffany Trump by his second wife, Marla Maples.

Donald Trump's father, Fred, was born in New York City and became one of the biggest real estate developers in the city. Fred and his mother Elizabeth founded Elizabeth Trump and Son, a real estate firm which Donald renamed The Trump Organization and served as its chairman and president until he became President of the United States.

Donald Trump's mother, Mary Anne MacLeod Trump was born in Scotland, the daughter of a fisherman. At age 17 she immigrated to New

York and started working as a maid. Mary met Fred in New York and married him in 1936. She became a U.S. citizen in 1942.

Donald Trump's grandfather, Frederick Trump, immigrated in 1885 from Killstadt, Bavaria, to the United States at age 16. In 1892 he became a U.S. citizen. During the Klondike Gold Rush, he amassed a fortune by opening restaurants and hotels for gold seekers on their way to the region. After his death, his fortune was passed on to his wife and son. Frederick Trump was a second cousin of Henry J. Heinz, founder of H. J. Heinz Company.

Donald Trump's grandmother, Elizabeth Christ Trump was born in 1880 in Killstadt, Bavaria, and moved from there to the United States. She married Frederick in 1902. She was the matriarch of the Trump family.

Donald Trump's paternal uncle, John George Trump, was an electrical engineer, inventor and physicist who with Robert J. Van de Graff, developed rotational radiation therapy which was one of the first million-volt x-ray generators. He was a recipient of The Ronald Reagan National Medal of Science and a member of the National Academy of Engineering.

Donald Trump's elder sister is a retired judge of The United States Court of Appeals for the Third Circuit.[11]

---

[11] Information obtained from, *"The Family of Donald Trump,"* by *Wikipedia* on March 10, 2017.

CHAPTER 13

August 17 2016

It Didn't Take Long For a

Trump Change in Campaign Leadership

Stephen Bannon and Kellyanne Conway

The Trump campaign announced that *Breitbart News* Chief, Stephen Bannon, was taking a leave of absence to become the Chief Executive of the Trump campaign immediately and Kelleyanne Conway would be the campaign manager. Recent polls show Trump having problems in five key states of Florida, North Carolina, Virginia, Ohio and Pennsylvania. These states are considered critical for Trump to carry if he is to win the election. Several polls show Trump behind 6 to 9 points in these states.

Why would Trump appoint Steve Bannon as an assistant to the President and his Chief Strategist?

First, let's examine his educational background. He received a BS degree from Virginia Tech in urban planning. He holds a master's degree in National Security Studies from Georgetown University School of Foreign Service. He received a Master of Business Administration degree with honors from Harvard Business School. He served seven years in the U S Navy as a Surface Warfare Officer and as a special assistant to the Chief of Naval Operations at the pentagon. Bannon is considered an ultra-conservative. After his naval career, he worked at Goldman Sachs as an investment banker where he worked in the acquisitions and mergers field. He specialized in the media area. He negotiated the sale of Castle Rock Entertainment Company to Ted Turner and as payment accepted a financial stake in five television shows one of which was Seinfeld. He went on to become an executive producer making 18 films. In 2012 he became executive chairman of Breitbart News, LLC. On August 16, 2016 he left this position to go to work for the Trump campaign. After the election, Trump appointed him to attend all meetings of the (NSC) National Security Council.

Kelleyanne Conway, a political activist, strategist and former president and CEO of the Polling Company worked for the Ted Cruz campaign until he quit the race. On July 1, 2016, Trump appointed her as senior adviser to his campaign. On August 19, 2016 Paul Manafort resigned as campaign manager and Trump elevated her to this position, which she held for the balance of the election.

She became the first woman to successfully run a presidential campaign. On December 22, 2016 president-elect Trump appointed her as Counselor to the President, a position she currently holds.

Conway received a B.A. magna cum laude in political science from Trinity Washington University, where she was elected to Phi Beta Kappa. She then earned a Doctor of Jurisprudence degree with honors from George Washington University Law School.

Conway has worked with Laura Ingraham, Ann Coulter and other conservative television commentators in the cable television industry. She has represented Congressman Jack Kemp, Senator Fred Thompson, House Speaker Newt Gingrich and Congressman Mike Pence, now the Vice-President. She is considered a communications pro and an expert in conducting accurate polls having worked for American Express, ABC News and *Ladies Home Journal*. Regarding her polling activities, she has appeared on ABC, CBS, NBC, PBS, CNN, MSNBC and the Fox News Channel.

What happened to Manafort, and why did he resign two days after Bannon and Conway appeared on the scene? Manafort's personal business dealings had become an issue as it was reported that he accepted $12 million in undisclosed cash payments from Ukraine President Viktor Yanukovych's political party. It has also been reported that Manafort had ties to the Kremlin. The attention was focused on Manafort rather than

Trump, and Trump decided that this was an unacceptable distraction to him winning the election.

I believe the main reason Manafort was replaced was because of the poll numbers which showed Trump falling behind so badly that he might not recover in time to win on November 8, 2016. [12]

Actually, both of these individuals played a key role in the Trump victory. Bannon remained in the background advising him privately while Conway became a very public figure perhaps persuading many women to vote for Trump. She has been called, "The secret weapon who won the War, aka "The Trump Whisperer." It is said that her words resonated with white suburban women across America. [13] More than 53% of the white women in America voted for Trump with Conway playing a large role in this achievement.

More than 94% of the black women and 68% of the Latina women voted for Hillary. [14]

I believe this change in campaign management was significantly important in the outcome of this election. Trump was behind and the trend showed him losing badly until this change.

After this change, the poll numbers began to improve dramatically. One of the main reasons was Conway appeared on television constantly singing the praises of Trump.

On March 15, 2017, I was looking on the internet when I saw a tape by Steve Bannon who credits Kellyanne Conway with Trump winning the election. He said that after the tape of Trump's lewd conversation was published, Kellyanne went on national TV and supported Trump's sincere apology and suggested that people should forgive him and vote for him. [15]

---

[12] Information from, "*The Guardian.*"

[13] Information from, "*The Guardian.*"

[14] This information furnished by: "*Popsugar.*" November 30, 2016 article by Laura Levinson

[15] *Geobeats* furnished the information for this comment dated March 15, 2017.

CHAPTER 14

August 19, 2016

State Department Admits Obama Lied

$400 Million Cash Payment was Contingent

On Prisoner Release

Ransom is Alive and Well

How $400 Million turns into $3.4 Billion

In the summer of 2016, President Obama said there was no connection between the $400 Million cash payment to Iran and the release of prisoners held by them. This was confirmed by John Kirby, spokesperson for the State Department. Then *The Wall Street Journal* talked with one of the released prisoners who reported that the plane they were on in Iran was held for over 20 hours with an Iranian official saying that the plane could not leave until another plane arrived. That was the plane with the $400 Million in cash that was not supposed to be contingent on the release of the prisoners. Then John Kirby, State Department spokesperson, said the release of the prisoners was contingent upon the payment of the $400 million. So it appeared the U.S. did in fact pay a ransom for the prisoners in conflict with what President Obama had previously told the American people. Obama was outraged that the press would even question the transaction saying again the U.S. does not pay a ransom. The truth was we have learned the U.S. would not let Iran take control of the plane on the ground carrying the cash until the plane carrying the hostages was allowed to leave Tehran on January 17, 2016. We now know this was a tightly scripted exchange timed to the release of the American prisoners held in Iran. This information was based on the accounts of several U.S. officials. Would this lead Iran to seize any American they can find and demand cash payment for their release? Ransom is alive and well.

Did I say $400 million? Let's try 3 billion 400 million in total. On September 7, 2016, our government sent $400 million in cash with each of the two other plane-load installments coming soon after the first payment! The other two payments of $1.3 billion were flown to Iran not on January 17, 2016, but on January 22 and February 5, 2016. The currency is not traceable and was sent in Swiss Francs, Euros and other currencies. The world's leading state sponsor of terror received pallets of cash, and we had no idea where the cash would end up, or do we? Some believe the money was going to their military to fund their terrorist network. Were any protections put into the agreement with Iran to impose punishments for seizing Americans and holding them for ransom? No such limits have been announced. Why not?

Hillary supported President Obama's position on these events. It was Obama's position that the payment was in settlement of a 1979 dispute between the U.S. and Iran over Iran's money that the U.S. froze after the hostage crisis. The U.S. admits that the timing of the payment was tied to getting our prisoners released from Iran. Iran called it a ransom payment while Obama called it a settlement.

What will the people call it in November?

CHAPTER 15

August 19, 2016

Flood Disaster in Louisiana

The worst natural disaster since hurricane Sandy four years ago hit the state of Louisiana in August of 2016. Thousands of people lost everything they owned according to the Red Cross. It is estimated that the cost will run over $30 billion. In Livingston Parish, more than 31 inches of rain fell in 15 hours. This is a rate of over 2 inches of rain every hour for 15 hours. At least 13 people died across 5 parishes and more than 30,000 people had to be rescued from the floods. More than 110,000 homes having a value of 21 billion were in the region that flooded.

All of this was going on while Obama was playing golf on vacation. He had refused to cut his vacation short to go to the region. Into this event came Donald Trump and Mike Pence to make a visit to Louisiana and purchase a truck load of supplies for the flood victims and then distribute them to the needed flood victims. The governor of Louisiana told Trump not to come for a photo op, but to volunteer to help and make a contribution for the flood victims. So that is what happened.[16]

Hillary posted a memo on "Facebook," saying she won't be going to Louisiana because she doesn't want to interfere with the relief work that is going on there. She called on her supporters to make donations to help the people recover from this terrible disaster. [17]

---

[16] This information furnished by CNN
[17] This information furnished by *USA Today*

Some say this move by Trump was just a publicity stunt to get votes. Others say Trump really cares about these people and came to help them. The voters will give us the answer in November! [18]

If this was nothing but a publicity stunt, the people of Louisiana saw it differently. A 20% point win is a substantial margin in any voter's book.

---

[18] This chapter was written in late August, 2016. As a follow up after the election, it is interesting to see that Trump carried Louisiana with 1,178,638 votes, or 58% to Hillary's 780,154 votes, or 38%.

Data taken from the certified results of Louisiana as published in the New York Times.

CHAPTER 16

August 22, 2016

New Emails from FBI Appear

The FBI announced that it had recovered an additional 14,900 emails from Hillary's private server that had not been previously disclosed by her attorneys. The emails were turned over to the State Department. U.S. District Judge James E. Boasberg pressed the State Department to begin releasing the contents sooner than mid-October as planned.[19] These records were among the tens of thousands of documents found by the FBI and turned over to the State Department according to their attorneys. The problem appeared to be the 14,900 emails were approximately 50% more than the roughly 30,000 emails that Clinton's attorneys deemed work-related and returned to the State Department in December 2014. The emails revealed a close relationship between the State Department and the Clinton Foundation. It appeared that many people were making contributions to the Clinton Foundation to gain access to Hillary when she was Secretary of State. The question to be determined was whether these contributors to the Clinton Foundation got more than access when they contributed and met with Hillary. We now know that 85 of the154 persons who met with Hillary contributed $156 million to The Clinton Foundation. At least 40 donated more than a $100,000 each and 20 gave more than $1million each. The Clinton Foundation has raised more than $2 billion since its creation in 2000. The investigation continues into what they got for their money.[20]

---

[19] Information from, "*The Washington Post.*"

[20] Information obtained from *The Washington Post* and *The Associated Press*

The emails revealed that the requests for a meeting with Secretary Clinton were handled by Huma Abedin, who consulted with Hillary and other top officials on how to respond to the request.

So far there is no evidence that the donors got any more than a meeting for their donation, but the investigation continues and remains a cloud over Hillary's campaign.

Trump called for Hillary to totally shut down the foundation calling it one of the most corrupt enterprises in political history.

Knowing 40 people gave more than $100,000.00 each and 20 gave more than $1millon each, the main question is why would a person give this kind of money and what did they expect to get in return? We may never know the answers to these questions. Many people believed that for such contributions something special was expected. Was Hillary using a private server to hide these emails so they would not appear in the records of the State Department, or be turned over to the FBI or the public? Could it be that these contributors were thinking that when Hillary got to the white house, she would give them special access to her? This type of conduct does not pass the smell test, meaning this behavior stinks! This is just another reason why some people believe we have the finest politicians money can buy!

The Clinton's raised $2 billion in 16 years. That amounts to $125 million per year, every year for 16 years. Let's take the year 2013 for an example, as it appears that only about 6% to 7% of the total contributions of 140 million or about $9 million went for direct aid. They spent $84 million on functional expenses with about $64 million left over. The experts say a good charity spends about 75% of its funds on direct aid. *So much for the charity idea!*

Bill Allison, a senior fellow at Sunlight Foundation, a governmental watchdog group described The Clinton Foundation as operating as a slush fund for the Clintons rather than as a charity.[21]

How would this affect the voters? My personal opinion was the more questionable behavior we found out about, the more harmful it would be to Hillary's chances of winning in November. This type of conduct made Hillary look dishonest in the eyes of the average American voter and led to a great amount of distrust!

---

[21] Information obtained from "*The New York Post*," in an article by Hannah Withlam dated February 23, 2017.

CHAPTER 17

Trump Says to African-Americans "What in the Hell do you Have to Lose?"

When Trump asked this question, he was trying to appeal to the African-American and Hispanic vote. His new manager and adviser had told him he must improve his numbers among women, Hispanics and African-Americans, if he was to win the election. At the beginning of October, 2016, the polls showed only 9% of the African-Americans supported Trump. [22]

In a speech Trump talked about the high unemployment rate for African-Americans and Hispanic citizens. The crime rate is high in these communities, and the poor quality of schools is leading to many problems. These citizens have been promised many improvements in the past by the Democrats, but the Democrats have failed to deliver on their promises. So the idea was that Trump was justified in asking this question. Trump was promising better schools, jobs and increased police protection for their communities, so they can walk down their streets without getting shot. The main question was whether these citizens will listen to him and decide to vote for him. Only time will tell.

Oct 3-9%
Oct 6-12%
Oct 7 - 13%
Oct 10- 14%

---

[22] *The Rasmussen Poll* in October reveals some interesting data regarding minority voters for Trump:

Oct 11- 19%
Oct 12- 19%
Oct 13- 24%

In 10 days Trump's polling numbers increased by 16% points. Then look what happened for the next 9 days.

Oct 17- 17%
Oct 18- 19%
Oct 19- 18%
Oct 20- 15%
Oct 21- 16%
Oct 24 – 15%
Oct 25 – 16%

Trump's polling numbers decreased by 8 % points.

The African-Americans make up 22 % of the Democratic vote.

If the Democrats lost just 25% of the black vote, they would lose Virginia, Florida, Ohio and North Carolina. The last three of these states are considered critical to a Trump win.

"*The Washington Post*," made the following observation: "If Trump skims 25% of the black votes from the Democratic Party, he would win the 2016 election in a landslide."

My thinking is that the Trump campaign knew Hillary was going to get the great majority of the minority vote, but Trump figured that any of these votes he could get would simply hurt Hillary's numbers so it was worth a try to skim a few votes away from her.

After the election the final analysis reveals that Hillary got 88% of the black vote and Trump only got 8%, but the real story was that the blacks did not turn out and vote in large numbers to overcome the bigger white vote that Trump got.[23]

---

[23] The *CBS News* Exit

CHAPTER 18

The Large Unfavorable Rating
for Both Candidates

After the Democratic convention, Hillary got a boost in the polls and maintained a large lead in the National polls and in many of the states that were toss-ups. The national polls generally showed Clinton with a 48% to Trump's 41% lead in late July after the conventions. Various other polls showed Clinton leading by as little as 3% to as much as 10% nationally. It is interesting to note that after the first debate of September 26, 2016, Hillary also got a boost in the polls. She got a sharp increase in independent support going to 44% for her to 37% for Trump. Regarding men, she went from a 22% deficit to only down 5%, for a substantial change in the way men viewed her as president. The national survey showed:

Clinton 47%

Trump 42%

Johnson 7%

Stein 2%

The key states of North Carolina, Florida, Pennsylvania and Ohio were too close to call and remained the key to the election according to the experts.

Considering their favorability rating, Trump had fallen from 54% (favor) to 59% (unfavorable) while Hillary had remained at 43% (favor) to 54% (unfavorable).

We still had a unique situation where the voters had an unfavorable opinion of both candidates.[24]

---

[24] Information from CNN

CHAPTER 19

September 1, 2016

More Problems for Hillary

Guess What? You paid for Hillary's Private Server

It has been revealed that Bill Clinton, as he was building the Clinton Foundation into a $2 billion charity (or enterprise depending on your view of this situation) spent $16 million in taxpayer funds to pay some of the expenses of the Clinton Foundation and to fund the purchase of the equipment and the private server that went with the equipment, all of which was housed at the Clinton Foundation to be used by and for Hillary. The Clintons also used these same funds to fund salaries and benefits of several aides, who were now at the center of the email problem. Was this legal? Yes, under an old program designed to keep a former president out of the poorhouse, Congress passed the Former President Act. Clinton aides also got the (GSA) Government Services Administration to pay for computer technology used partly by the Clinton Foundation.

I'm not sure that Congress intended for a former president to use these funds to benefit a $2 billon foundation, but apparently it was legal.[25]

It was also discovered that 13 of the 22 staffers who had been paid by the GSA to work for President Bill Clinton's personal office also worked for The Clinton Foundation. One of these staffers was Justin Cooper whose

---

[25] Information obtained from *The National Review Magazine* article by Jim Geraghty dated September 1, 2016.

salary was supplemented to the tune of $10,000.00 and who, without any security clearance or security training, helped set up a private email account that Hillary could use to send and receive classified information as Secretary of State. Her use of this system has been described as "Extremely careless," by James Comey, Director of the FBI. Cooper continued working to maintain Hillary's private email system through 2012 including advising her top aides, Huma Abedin and Cheryl Mills, on attempted hacks. It was during this time that Cooper was on a GSA payroll drawing a federal government stipend from February 2012 through 2013. Also at this same time Cooper was working with Doug Bland, another Clinton trusted lieutenant, to launch a global consulting firm called Tenco. This firm did lucrative work for foundation donors and entities with business before Clinton's State Department. Tenco also paid Huma Abedin as a senior advisor. [26]

The questions must be asked: Why didn't the $2 billion foundation pay for these expenses and how can these expenses be justified as an expense to be paid for by you and me as taxpayers? Are they accountable to anyone? Yes, they are only accountable to the voters on November 8, 2016. Will the people elect her to serve in the most powerful position in this country?

So here we have a situation where the Clintons have done certain things that were legal, but they sure don't look very good to the average voter. It appears that this is an abuse of power by Bill Clinton, especially when there is a lot of money in the foundation to pay for these expenses.

---

[26] Information obtained from "*Politico Magazine* article by Kenneth P. Vogel Dated September 1, 2016.

CHAPTER 20

39 Responses of "I do not recall"

Is Hillary Mentally and Physically Fit to Serve as President

FBI Releases Notes from Hillary Interview

September 2, 2016

On Friday, September 2, 2016, just before the long Labor Day weekend, the FBI released notes of the interview it conducted with Hillary on July 2, 2016. Hillary told the FBI she did not recall the briefing she received on handling sensitive information due to a concussion suffered in 2012. She said she received no instructions or directions regarding the preservation or production of State Department records. State Department employees told the FBI that many emails from Hillary appeared to be from "H" and did not show her private email domain. The notes reflect that Hillary told the FBI "She did not recall," in answer to 39 questions regarding her use of a private server and the emails sent or received. We learned that she used 13 different devices (phones) when communicating with others. She had previously told the American people that she used 2 phones, but never mentioned the other phones or 5 iPads she had used. Many of these devices have not been recovered, but one phone that was recovered was destroyed by the use of a hammer. Hillary tried to blame Colin Powell for the use of her email system, but Powell said he warned her that she should only use her system for non-business and non- confidential material, as the business material would become the property of the government as part of her official record. Many of the devices she used have been lost or destroyed so the information on these systems has not been recovered.[27]

The notes from the interview leave many questions that need to be answered. Was the interview recorded or a court reporter present to take down what was said so that a transcript could be provided for future reference? CNN reported that the interview was not recorded or taped. A court reporter did not take down the testimony. Who was present in the room during the interview, and why were they there? This information was not revealed. Who was in charge of the process? Why did the FBI wait until Friday before a long holiday weekend to disclose this information?

Her answers to the FBI questions also made us wonder if she was still suffering from her concussion and had a serious memory loss. A better answer to these issues might come as we got closer to the election and Hillary furnished medical information on her condition.

As a former prosecutor I wondered if she was using, "I don't recall," as an excuse for covering up the real answer, or was she really suffering from memory loss due to a former concussion suffered in 2012. That was four years ago which led me to think that she had some kind of permanent brain damage or memory problem that had not been corrected. If this was the case, we certainly didn't want her having to deal with the daily stress of running this country or making very difficult decisions on a daily basis. A brain damaged president does not need to be placed in the situation of having to decide if we need to start a nuclear war or defend against one.

---

[27] Information obtained from CNN report by Tal Kopan and Evan Perez dated September 2, 2016

CHAPTER 21

Here Comes WikiLeaks Again

September 6, 2016

Julian Assange, founder of WikiLeaks, said that Hillary was lying when she said she did not know what the classified "C" marker used in government email correspondence during her time in the state department meant. She told the FBI she could not remember what the "C" meant. Assange showed Sean Hannity of Fox News that Hillary had used the "C" herself in many of her emails and had received many thousands of emails with the use of "C" in them.

John Schindler writing in the *New York Observer Politics* indicated that the documents released show that Hillary is dishonest, thoroughly incompetent and is utterly clueless about classification matters. Schindler is a former NSA analyst, counterintelligence officer, a specialist in espionage and terrorism, Naval Officer and War College Professor. He went on to say that Hillary shows an ignorance that is shocking, considering that she is a former top official of our government and wants to be our next commander-in-chief. All government workers are required to take the classification course, but Hillary did not attend this course, so it is not surprising that she has no idea what she is talking about when discussing the classification system. The system is simple: the symbols C, S and TS stand for confidential, secret and top secret. His conclusion was if Hillary is this dumb, she is nowhere near smart enough to be our commander-in-chief. She was asked about drone strikes which were considered top secret and part of the super-sensitive Special Access Program. Her response indicated that she had no clue as to the sensitivity of this information and stated that it would be permitted for this type information to be contained on an unclassified system. The FBI investigation determined that she sent hundreds of emails containing classified information on her unclassified Blackberry phone while traveling in many countries, including Russia. They presumed that these countries now have this information since it was not protected. We now know that Hillary had a habit of losing her electronic devices- as many as 13 went missing. In two cases a member of the Clinton staff tried to destroy the phone with a hammer which does not prevent a competent spy service from getting the classified information off of them.[28]

Was Hillary dishonest, incompetent, brain damaged, still suffering from a concussion after 4 years, ignorant about classified information, dumb or simply trying to avoid prosecution by giving an answer that kept her from being indicted? Well, it really didn't matter because whichever one or more of these excuses was the actual answer, it still led me to conclude that she did not need to be anywhere near the oval office.

What will the voters think regarding Hillary's competency? We will find out in November.

---

[28] Information furnished by WikiLeaks and John Schindler of *the New York Political Observer.*

CHAPTER 22

9-11-2016

Hillary's Medical Condition

The latest Polls

During a memorial service for the victims of 9-11, Hillary got "overheated," and had to leave. The early morning visit revealed that the temperature was about 80 degrees and Hillary became unstable in her walk, lost her shoe, fell and had to be lifted into her van, and she was taken to her daughter's home to recover. No journalists were allowed to be with her during this time, and about two hours later, she reappeared and said she was fine and feeling great. We found out on Friday she was diagnosed with pneumonia, which was not disclosed to the public until Monday.

Once again, Hillary had a credibility issue by not telling the truth. On Sunday afternoon the internet was filled with questions regarding her health and some people were wondering if she should be replaced due to her health. Joe Biden seems to be waiting in the background ready to fill in for Hillary, if she was removed or dropped out due to health reasons.

The latest CNN poll showed that Hillary's lead had disappeared. Trump now led by two points. Hillary had an 8 point lead around two weeks ago and appeared to be pulling away, but that seemed to be changing in spite of the fact that she had spent around $125 million on TV ads compared to less than $25 million Trump spent. *The Associated Press* reported that more than one-half of the people who had meetings with her when she was Secretary of State also donated to the Clinton Foundation. *The New York Times* also reported several articles revealing the cozy ties between the Clinton Foundation and the State Department. Then to add gas to the fire, the FBI released the interview notes taken when she talked to the FBI about her handling of classified material while she conducted official State Department business on her private email server. Ashe Cowe, writing for the *Observer,* concluded that Hillary was either truly incompetent (and should be nowhere near the oval office) or was a corrupted liar and she might very well be both.[29]

Would the best approach be to tell the public: "I've come down with a case of pneumonia? I'm going to follow my doctor's orders and take a few days off to get some rest. I'll be back on the campaign trail in a few days."

It seemed to me that Hillary often failed to exercise good judgment, thus creating serious problems for her becoming president. Why not tell the people the truth? When you cover up or attempt to hide the truth, it makes some folks wonder what else you are concealing.

---

[29] Information obtained from the *"The Washington Post."*

CHAPTER 23

New polls in Four Swing States
September 15, 2016

The alleged experts were saying that the race will be determined by the four swing states of Florida, North Carolina, Ohio and Pennsylvania. Some experts said Trump must have all 4 states to win the race, so let's take a look at the polls in these four states as of September 15. We were 54 days from Election Day.

Trump had now taken a 3 point lead in Florida- 46% to Hillary's 43% according to the latest CNN poll. Just a short time ago Hillary had the lead in Florida by 5% Points.

In Ohio, according to CNN, Trump had taken a 5 point lead over Hillary with Trump showing 46 % to Hillary's 41%. Hillary had previously had the lead by several points.

In North Carolina, Trump led 42% to Hillary's 38%. Again, this represented a change in the lead.

In Pennsylvania, Trump led 48% to 43%, a lead change from last week.

Other polls showed major changes. In Iowa, a Monmouth University Poll showed Trump with an 8 point lead over Hillary, while Nevada showed Trump with a 2 point lead.

Trump had taken a lead in the latest national poll revealing Trump 46% to Clinton 45%. [30]

What was going on to cause such an important change in these key states? Nearly half of the American people were very concerned about two

---

[30] Information furnished by CNN

issues that have hounded Hillary, which many believed were the cause of the changes in these states:

1. The use of a private email server to conduct official State Department business containing confidential information that may have been hacked by others.
2. Contributions made to the Clinton Foundation by foreign governments, foreign and domestic corporations and others to get special favors from Hillary when she was Secretary of State. Many believe 33,000 emails were destroyed to cover up the favors granted by Hillary.

It will be interesting to see if this trend continues.

Fifty-four days in politics is a very long time and, in fact, too long to count on things not changing. This race had so many issues involving two extremely controversial candidates and the outcome could go down to the last few days. I thought there were many people still undecided who might not vote for either candidate.

CHAPTER 24

September 13, 2016

Trump Goes After the Woman Vote

Childcare

Speaking in Aston, Pennsylvania, Trump rolled out his child care policy in an appeal to increase his votes from women. It was believed Trump had significant input from his daughter, Ivanka, who has three children and was a high ranking executive in the Trump Organization. Also contributing to the plan was Trump's campaign manager, Kellyanne Conway, who is the mother of four children. The plan called for ensuring 6 weeks of paid maternity leave and lowering child care cost by making it tax deductible for up to four children and elderly dependents. Hillary's plan called for 12 weeks of paid maternity leave.

Also included in Trump's proposal were additional spending rebates through the Earned Income Tax Credit, expanded deduction opportunities for stay-at-home parents and revised federal savings accounts to set aside funds for child development and educational needs.[31]

However, some people believed the proposal to make all childcare costs tax deductible would boost the bottom line for wealthier parents, but deliver little benefit to working parents at the lower end of the income ladder. Why? Those at the lower end of the income bracket don't make enough to pay income taxes so this plan would be of little benefit to them. It seemed that all people agreed that something must be done to help with

---

[31] Information obtained from "*The Washington Post*," article of September 13, 2016 by Sean Sullivan and Robert Costa.

child care cost because it often acts as a barrier to women going to work. Another problem for both proposals is that you only get the benefit long after you incur the expense. [32]

At this time I thought Trump must do something to appeal to the women, especially those who needed to work but couldn't earn enough money to afford the childcare expenses they would incur when working. His comments about women had been so insulting that many had said they would not vote for him. Many said they would not vote for Hillary either. So how many people will vote in the election, but will not vote in the presidential race?

What was going on to cause such an unusual voting pattern?

After the election, the results showed the following:

Forty per cent or about 93 million of the eligible voters did not vote at all, which leaves 126 million who did. The data showed that out of those 126 million who did vote, there were 2,395,271who did not vote in the presidential race.[33]

Trump carried Wisconsin, Michigan and Pennsylvania by a combined total of only 107,000 votes. Trump carried Michigan by 11,837 votes. Trump carried Wisconsin by 27,257 votes.[34]

These three states were critically important in Trump getting the needed Electoral College votes to put him over the top.

Did women vote for Trump? Hillary carried 54% of the women voters compared with Trump's 42%. However, Trump outperformed Hillary among white women, winning 53% of those voters. Trump beat Hillary among white women without college degrees by 27 points. In three of the states that decided the election- Wisconsin, Pennsylvania and Michigan-that margin was enough to send Trump to the White House.[35]

---

[32] CBS Money Watch News: Program by Kate Gibson of August 8, 2016.

[33] Information furnished by "*Heavy*," in article by Daniel S. Levine dated November 10, 2106.

[34] Information furnished by "*Heavy*," in article by Daniel S. Levine dated November 10, 2106.

[35] Information obtained from "*The Vox,*" in an article by Tara Tolshan dated January 21, 2017.

CHAPTER 25

Trumps Tax Plan

As far as individuals are concerned, Trump proposed 3 tax rate brackets of 12%, 25% and 33%, with an enlarged standard deduction of $15,000.00 for individuals and $30,000.00 for joint filers, under which 60% fewer people would itemize their tax deduction. The estate tax would be repealed and in its place capital gains would be taxed at death with an exemption of around $10 million.

For businesses and the rich, Trump planned for a huge tax cut with an emphasis on growth. It would inject $4-6 trillion into the economy over a 10 year period by means of business tax cuts. Trump wanted to lower the corporate income tax rate to 15% and make it available to half of all U.S. businesses that are not in the corporate form. Trump wanted a proposed repatriation at a 10% rate for cash and 4% for earnings not represented by cash.[36]

Foreign profits held overseas by U.S. Corporations to avoid taxes at home nearly doubled from 2008 to 2013 to top nearly 2.1 trillion. These profits are not taxed until brought into the U.S. and there is a move to encourage U.S. companies to return these profits to the U.S. at a reduced tax rate. The current corporate tax rate of 35% discourages most corporations from bringing these profits into the U.S. It's indicated Trump's plan will certainly propose a method of bringing this money back into the U.S. so it can be taxed at a lower rate and used to boost our economy by adding jobs to workers in America.[37]

---

[36] Information furnished by *"Forbes,"* in article of November 13, 2016 by Lee Sheppard.

[37] Information furnished by *"Reuters,"* in article of April 8, 2014.

CHAPTER 26

September 19, 2016

Hundreds of Immigrants Wrongly Granted Citizenship

The U.S. government mistakenly granted citizenship to at least 858 immigrants who had pending deportation orders from countries of concern to national security or with high rates of immigration fraud, according to an internal Homeland Security audit. The Inspector General found that the immigrants used different names or birthdates to apply for citizenship and such discrepancies were not caught because their fingerprints were missing from the government database. The problem resulted from old paper-based records containing fingerprint information that couldn't be searched electronically. Immigration officials are in the process of uploading these files, and officials will review every file identified as a possible case of fraud. Fingerprints are missing from federal databases for as many as 315,000 immigrants with final deportation orders, or who are fugitive criminals. The government has known about the gap in the records since 2008, but few cases have been investigated.

The consequences of granting citizenship to someone who has been ordered deported are very serious because these U. S. citizens can now apply and receive security clearances or take security-sensitive jobs. The Inspector General found that one of these citizens was now a law enforcement officer and three had been hired in the aviation industry where they had access to secure areas at airports and maritime facilities and vessels.[38]

Thus, we see that there may be far reaching and seriously dangerous consequences to having records that are not up to date. The security of our nation is at stake and our lawful citizens are at risk. We have known about this problem since 2008. We have had 8 years to correct this problem, but nothing has been done. It is far past time to correct mistakes like this especially since there are many illegal immigrants who may want to get in positions where they can do our people great harm. Who's looking out after the people?

Trump says he will protect the people and the huge crowds at his rallies seem to believe him.

---

[38] Information obtained from "*The Associated Press*," article by Alicia A. Caldwell dated September 19, 2016.

CHAPTER 27

Trump's Outrageous Statements

Trump was guilty of making some outrageous statements during his campaign. Many of these statements had nothing to do with the run for the presidency, but were aimed at segments of the population that one would think he needed to vote for him. It is interesting to look at a few of them.

"One of the key problems today is that politics is such a disgrace. Good people don't go into government."

"I could stand in the middle of 5th avenue and shoot someone and I wouldn't lose any voters."

"If Ivanka weren't my daughter, perhaps I'd be dating her."

"I think the only difference between me and the other candidates is that I'm more honest and my women are better looking."

"Ariana Huffington is unattractive, both inside and out. I fully understand why her former husband left her for a man- he made a good decision."

"If I were running "The View," I'd fire Rosie O'Donnell. I mean, I'd look at her right in that fat, ugly face of hers, I'd say, Rosie, you're fired."

"When Mexico sends its people, they're not sending their best…They're bringing drugs. They're bringing crime. They're rapists."

"I have a great relationship with Mexican people."

"How stupid are the people of Iowa"?

"We can't continue to allow China to rape our country."

"The point is you can't be too greedy."

"Obama has no solutions. Obama has failed the country and its great citizens, and they don't like it when I speak the truth about this- it hurts too much."

"John McCain is not a war hero. He just got captured." (John McCain spent 5 years in a Vietnam prison camp in Hanoi, after he was captured.)

"I can grope and kiss beautiful women because I am rich and famous. When you are a star, the women let you do anything."

These are only a few of the surprising statements Trump made during his race for the presidency. Many voters got upset at these comments and indicated that they would never vote for Trump.

Many of these comments appear to be unnecessary and support the idea that Trump is unsteady and erratic. Some of these statements were made about events years ago and it's well known that Trump is a dedicated family man. Obviously, he has transformed some of his previous behaviors. He needed to focus on the issues and stop making statements that will come back to haunt him on Election Day.

CHAPTER 28

The Latest Polls

September 24, 2016

In the general election, the *Bloomberg Poll* showed a tie. In a two way race, Hillary and Trump were tied at 46% each. Hillary had dropped 4% while Trump had gained 2% in a nation-wide poll. Why? Young voters under 35 showed a 19% loss for Hillary. In August, Hillary had 29% of their vote. She now had 10%. The polls show they do not trust her.

In a four way race, the *Bloomberg Poll* had Hillary at 43%, Trump at 41%, Johnson at 8% and Stein at 4%. *The Washington Post*/ABC News poll showed Hillary at 46%, Trump at 44%, Johnson at 5% and Stein at 3%. In this poll Hillary's poll remained unchanged from August with Trump gaining 3%, Johnson loosing 4% and Stein loosing 1%.

The state polls showed Trump gaining ground on Hillary. *The Muhlenberg College Pennsylvania poll* had Hillary at 40%, unchanged from August, Trump at 38%, gaining 6% since August, Johnson at 8%, losing 6% since August and Stein at 3%, losing 3% since August.

In Colorado, *the CBS News* poll showed Hillary at 40%, a loss of 15% in one month, Trump at 39%, Johnson at 7% and Stein at 2%. Colorado was considered safe at one point with this state having lots of Democrats and Latinos. Now it is in play.

In Virginia, *the CBS News* poll showed Hillary at 45%, a loss of 5% in one month, Trump at 37%, unchanged in August, Johnson at 7%, unchanged in August and Stein at 1%, a loss of 1% in one month.

Maine has 2 electoral votes that can be split in their 2 congressional districts. Hillary had 40%, Trump 37%, Johnson 12% and Stein 3%.[39]

So what is going on to make these changes? Had Trump become less controversial and more disciplined in his campaign? I think he had and it showed in these polls.

It appeared that Johnson and Stein would not reach the necessary votes to participate in the debate.

My guess was that Kelleyanne Conway and Stephen Bannon had a serious discussion with Trump. It appeared that both of them had told Trump to stop making controversial comments and focus on the issues or risk losing the election. The people wanted answers to important issues on jobs, the economy, immigration, stopping drugs from entering our country and how we were going to protect our citizens from those who would come here to hurt us. It appeared they had insisted Trump use a teleprompter and not go off script, which he was so inclined to do when he got all fired up in his rallies. The effect of discipline in his campaign speeches was noticeable to the people, and, as a result, he was gaining in the polls. Trump's temperament and steadiness had been an issue in the past, and it was time he displayed both to those voters who were still undecided and independents. Some had accused him of being erratic and inconsistent in his positions. The Bloomberg poll told us the race was tied at 46% for each candidate. It was about 6 weeks until the election so it was time to get serious and talk to the people about the issues like the outcome of this race depended on it, because it did. It was either candidate's race to win or lose. It was up to Trump to take their advice or lose the election.

---

[39] The information taken from the various polls mentioned as reported on news programs, NBC, CBS, ABC, Bloomberg, CNN, MSNBC, and Fox.

CHAPTER 29

The Three Debates

First: September 26, 2016

Second: October 9, 2016

Third: October 19, 2016

Who won the debates? Any Democrat would tell you that Hillary won the first one in a landslide. The Republicans said Trump missed some opportunities to "grill" Hillary, but he still won big. Ask the independents and they will tell you that no one won. It was a tie.

David Gergen expressed the opinion that Hillary won the first debate decisively, but she probably failed to put Trump away.[40]

However, S. E. Cupp expressed the opinion that Trump did the job he had to do.

It appeared that they both had some good points and they both missed some opportunities to score bigger wins.

In regards to the second debate, a CNN/ORC survey gave Hillary a 57 to 34 advantage with *YouGov* showing a closer margin of a win for Hillary 47 to 42.[41]

In the third debate, Clinton won by a thirteen point advantage 52 to

---

[40] *CNN* was the source of this information from program dated September 27, 2016.
[41] CNN/ORC and *Fortune Magazine* was the source of this information from an article by Troy Newmyer dated October 9, 2016.

39. This was due primarily to the fact that Trump was not sure he would accept the voter outcome of the election results. [42]

Hillary won the debates according to surveys taken by CNN/ORC and reported by *Fortune Magazine*. Either the CNN/ORC surveys were biased, were not a random sample, or the debates were not that important when the voters decided who to vote for on November 8, 2016.

---

[42] CNN/ORC and *Fortune Magazine* furnished this information in article dated October 19, 2016 by Troy Newmyer.

CHAPTER 30

September 29, 2016

The U S A Today Newspaper
Breaks a 34 Year Rule

In the 34 year history of *The USA Today* Newspaper, the Editorial Board had never taken sides in a presidential race. Until now! The paper was urging citizens not to vote for Trump. The Editorial Board said Trump was unfit to be president. Why? He does not have the temperament, knowledge, steadiness and honesty that America needs from its president. They questioned his support for our NATO allies, his opposition to Russian aggression, and whether he would honor payment of all of our debts. They believed he was erratic and had taken so many sides on so many issues that it was hard to know where he stood. His foreign policy ranged from uninformed to incoherent. The Wall Street Journal quoted Robert Gates, former Secretary of Defense, saying that Trump was "beyond repair." He trafficked in prejudice against Mexicans, Muslims and illegal immigrants. His business career was checkered with six bankruptcies, discrimination suits by blacks regarding housing rentals, misuse of his family charitable foundation, claims of fraud in his Trump University classes and lawsuits by small contractors and employees who were allegedly not paid for the work performed. The Board was concerned that Trump had not released his tax returns so they could determine his foreign financial entanglements, if any. He spoke recklessly by criticizing Gold Star parents who lost a son in Iraq or he mocked a disabled reporter. He invited Russian hackers to interfere with our American election by finding and publishing Hillary's missing emails. There were times that he made misstatements of facts, but rarely admitted he was wrong.

The paper went on to say they did not endorse Hillary either. The Board thought Trump was a bigger liar than Hillary, but admitted she had made many misstatements of facts. So the Board did not endorse anyone and simply suggested that each reader use their own judgment or maybe vote for one of the alternative candidates such as Gary Johnson of the Libertarian Ticket or Jill Stein of the Green Party.[43]

Since the paper did not endorse either candidate, there was not a great deal of harm done to either one of them.

---

[43] Information furnished by, "*The USA Today* Newspaper," dated September 29, 2016.

CHAPTER 31

The Washington Post Publishes
Crude Conversation Tape
October 9, 2016

NBC had knowledge of a 2005 taped conservation between Donald Trump and Billy Bush but refused to release it. *The Washington Post* decided to publish the contents in which Trump talks about wanting to kiss and grope women without their consent. He expressed his ideas as wanting to carry out these acts when he saw a beautiful woman. Trump said that when you are a star they let you do anything.

Trump and Billy Bush were in a bus on their way to tape a segment for *"Days of our Lives,"* when the recording was made. Trump told Bush about a time when he tried to seduce a woman whose name was not mentioned. Trump admitted that she was married and he moved on her very heavily. He even took her shopping for furniture hoping that would lead to an affair. Trump also stated that he was automatically attracted to beautiful women and could not control himself. He admitted, "I just start kissing them. It's like a magnet. I don't even wait." This conservation took place several months after Trump had married his third wife, Melania.

When the recording became public, Trump and Bush apologized for the crude remarks with Trump stating that these comments took place in 2005 and were not intended for public use. Trump insisted that he respects women and these tapes were 11 years old. He suggested that he had matured and changed in the past 11 years and also confirmed that he had apologized to Melania and members of his family. Hillary took advantage of this "horrific" event by indicating that Trump should not be elected President. Tim Cain said he got sick to his stomach when he heard the tape. Planned Parenthood said the tapes amounts to a sexual assault. House Speaker Paul Ryan said he was sickened by the tape and refused to appear on the campaign trail in Wisconsin with Trump. Many others expressed their disapproval of Trump's comments.

Many women were offended by those comments and decided to support Hillary. Several Republican politicians publicly withdrew their support for him even though Trump denied that he actually carried out these actions as compared to Bill Clinton who had actually raped several women. Then to make things worse, several women came forward to state that they had been sexually assaulted by Trump, being touched in places and ways that were inappropriate. [44]

Needless to say, this tape did not help Trump when it came to women, family values and the conduct of a newly married man. This conversation took place 11 years ago so it is not current, but it still hurts his image. Remember, appearance is critically important.

---

[44] Information furnished by, *"The Washington Post."*

CHAPTER 32

Who's Out to Get Trump?

Everybody!

Why don't we start with the Republican establishment, lobbyists, power brokers and the other Republican candidates? It was no secret that many of the established Republicans had refused to support Trump. His comment about it being time to "Drain the Swamp" had them scared they would lose their power and status as politicians who control the people. He defeated 17 candidates who wanted the nomination. Many of them spent millions of dollars that got them nowhere, and some refused to support the nominee even though they had promised to do so. This was before they woke up one day and realized that Trump might just get the nomination. They had not dreamed he would win the nomination and refused to take him seriously.

Next, let's look at the Democrats who all along said they wanted to run against Trump because they thought he would be the easiest candidate to beat. During the primary, Hillary often talked about Trump, lending fire to the idea that she wanted him to win the nomination. Once he got the nomination, it appeared that Hillary and her staff thought she would beat Trump by a wide margin. This idea was supported by the TV news media and the press, such as "*The Washington Post.*"

CNN (aka) Clinton News Network, MSNBC, NBC and BuzzFeed seemed to report favorably toward Hillary, while reflecting negatively on Trump. A survey revealed that some of these stations gave ten minutes in unfavorable coverage toward Trump to every minute of favorable coverage. It was rumored that Hillary set up and conducted a secret meeting with certain networks officials, but little is actually known about who attended the meeting or what was discussed at that time. It was evident that as the election neared, the TV networks were indicating a Hillary win with the polls confirming that she was in the lead and was going to win by a wide margin.

Were the polls correct or were they rigged as Trump stated? We may never know the answer to this question.

I believe there were many voters who had never voted before this election, who liked what Trump said and decided to vote for him. These people refused to publicly say who they were for, but expressed themselves on Election Day.

CHAPTER 33

The Affordable Healthcare Patient Act

Obamacare

The story of this election would not be complete without a chapter on The Affordable Healthcare Patient Act, better known as Obamacare. Hillary campaigned on the idea it should not be repealed, but possibly changed in some minor ways to make it better. Trump insisted that Obamacare had to be repealed and replaced with a totally new health care system that was more affordable and better.

Perhaps Bill Clinton said it better than anyone else when he campaigned for Hillary in Flint, Michigan on October 3, 2016 and said Obamacare was terrible for middle class Americans because they are penalized for not qualifying for government support. He pointed out the small business people and individuals were getting killed because they make just a little too much to get any of the subsidies available to others who make less, and the middle class was not organized and had no bargaining power. Bill Clinton went on to say that Obamacare was a "crazy system."

It appeared to me that Hillary tried to make the people believe that the system was working for most of the people, but I'm not sure the people agreed with that idea.

Trump jumped all over what Bill Clinton said, and at every rally he talked about how bad Obamacare was, that it was failing due to increased premiums, increased deductibles with many insurance companies refusing to provide coverage through the system.

Had the premiums increased? Let's take a look and see. New Mexico was asking for an average premium increase of 51.6%. Tennessee was seeking an average increase of 36.3%. Maryland was asking for an average increase of 30.4%. Oregon was asking for an average increase of 25%. These are just a few of the states reporting on increases, and these figures did not include the increase in deductibles that people would have to pay. It appeared that the Affordable Healthcare Patient Act was rapidly becoming unaffordable.

The Affordable Healthcare Patient Act was rushed into law and implemented with what now appears to have actuarial assumptions that were grossly defective regarding costs. Thus, the law should be reexamined to determine if costs can be reduced[45]

---

[45] Information furnished by, "*Breitbart*," in an article dated May 25, 2015, by Chriss W. Street.

CHAPTER 34

The 2016 Election Impacted

By

The United States Supreme Court Vacancy

Could this election be significantly influenced by vacancies on the Supreme Court? *It appears that the answer to this question is definitely yes.*

Let's look at the current make up of the court. Antonin Scalia, a conservative member of the court, passed away on February 13, 2016. The average age at which a Supreme Court justice retires is 78.7 years old. When the next president takes office, Justice Ruth Bader Ginsberg will be 83 years old; Justice Stephen Breyer will be 78 years old; Justice Anthony Kennedy will be 80 years old. This means the next president could be responsible for appointing four new justices on the court. Justices Ginsberg and Breyer are considered liberals, Scalia was a conservative, and Kennedy falls in the middle, but sides with the liberals about one-third of the time, often on social issues. Democrats usually appoint liberals to the court and Republicans appoint conservatives, each following the thinking of the president who appoints them. Thus, it seemed that the next president could impact the ideological nature of the court for many years to come, and this power was greatly coveted by both parties.[46]

There were several issues to be resolved before a vote of the Senate. President Obama had nominated Merrick Garland to fill the current

---

[46] *Ballotpedia,* Supreme Court Vacancy, 2017, An Overview.

vacant seat, but Senate Majority Leader Mitch McConnell had refused to allow the appointment to go forward to a vote in the Judiciary Committee or before the full Senate because the vacancy occurred during an election year. The Democrats were furious at McConnell and had promised to filibuster whoever the Republicans nominate if they won the White House.

A filibuster occurs when a legislator gives long speeches in an effort to delay or obstruct legislation that he or she opposes. It's important to remember that in 2013 the Democrats controlled the Senate, and they took a similar action.

If the Republicans didn't carry the Senate with 60 votes, then McConnell would have to change the rules of the Senate and exercise the nuclear option. The nuclear option is a parliamentary procedure that allows the U.S. Senate to override a rule or precedent by a simple majority of 51 votes, instead of by a supermajority of 60 votes.[47]

A book could be written on the importance of the Supreme Court in this election and its impact on our country. There are many issues which could be decided by the next Supreme Court and its composition could result in differing conclusions.

For example, the infamous Citizens United decision allowed corporations and unions to spend unlimited amounts of money, much of it "dark money," hidden from the public scrutiny. In the 2016 election, the Koch brothers announced that they and their friends would spend $889 million. This could lead to electing politicians more concerned with money than serving their electorate. It was believed that a liberal majority on the Supreme Court would overturn this decision.

In regard to election laws, the court has upheld state laws requiring a photo ID and proof of citizenship in order to register to vote in elections.

In regard to corporate laws, the court has upheld forced arbitration clauses regarding consumers and corporate workers, thus, denying them access to the judicial system.

In regard to gun control, the court has held that the Second Amendment applies to individuals, thus, making gun control much more difficult.

In regard to immigration, the court upheld a 5th Circuit Court of Appeals decision allowing as many as 5 million unauthorized immigrants, who were parents of citizens or of lawful permanent residents, to apply

---

[47] Wikipedia, Nuclear Option.

for a program that would spare them from deportation and provide them with work permits.

In regard to women's rights, the court has permitted companies to be exempt from having insurance to cover contraception based on the company's religious beliefs.

The court has rendered important decisions regarding discrimination, the right of prisoners to have DNA testing performed and health care.[48]

Did we know how much of an impact the vacancy would have on the 2016 election? Senate Majority Leader Mitch McConnell answered this question when he said on April 7, 2017, "President Trump might not have defeated Hillary Clinton in November had the Supreme Court not been a major issue in the 2016 campaign." He went on to say, "his decision to block former President Obama appointing a successor to the late Antonin Scalia was probably the decisive factor in Trump's win". [49]

---

[48] *Common Dreams* in an article dated July 29, 2016
[49] *The Washington Examiner,* in an article by David M. Drucker on April 7, 2017.

CHAPTER 35

Here Comes the FBI Again

11 Days Away from the Election

Early Friday afternoon, October 28, 2016, eleven days before the presidential election, James Comey, The Director of the FBI, sent a letter to Congressional leaders advising them that, due to newly discovered evidence obtained in a case involving Anthony Weiner, the FBI was reopening the investigation into the emails of Hillary Clinton. The FBI was examining the device belonging to Anthony Weiner when they came across his wife's emails which involved Hillary Clinton. The U.S. stock market dropped 150 points immediately. The attention of the entire nation was stopped to focus on the presidential election and the effect this new information would have on the outcome. Many states had early voting which meant millions of people had already cast their vote. So many questions remained unanswered due to the lack of details contained in the letter.

Trump immediately took advantage of the announcement to say maybe the election was not rigged as he had originally thought. Hillary made no mention of the situation in her Friday afternoon rally. She was 30 minutes late in her appearance for the event.

The news media went on a wild goose chase speculating whether the FBI had proof of criminal conduct. Could it be the evidence now showed that Hillary committed perjury when testifying before Congress? Did she obstruct justice when her emails were destroyed? Was there evidence that Hillary intentionally failed to protect national security by emailing classified, secret, or top secret information to people not cleared to receive such information? Would Hillary be denied top secret briefings based upon this new evidence?

Is a Grand Jury already impaneled to indict her before the election? Could it be that the American people were about to elect a person that would be an indicted felon? How long would it take the FBI to review the material so a statement could be made regarding her conduct? The nation awaited answers to these and many more questions and the media was having a field day. Could it be after reviewing this material, the FBI would not find the necessary evidence to indict Hillary? How would the people be able to make an informed decision on how they vote on Election Day if the FBI could not complete their work prior to the election?

Talk about chaos. When this information was blasted across the air waves, all the cable news networks and the other major networks filled the living rooms of America with nothing but this situation. It was not what I would call a quiet weekend.

The Democrats screamed "foul" as they said it was an improper comment to be made this close to the election. Some went so far as to say that Comey had broken the law by his comments. Hillary continued to insist that she had broken no laws and committed no crimes. Trump, who had claimed that the election was rigged, said that maybe the election was not rigged as he had first thought. Trump praised Comey for having the courage to finally say that the investigation should be reopened, implying that Hillary would finally be brought to justice. At his rallies he said that a vote for Hillary could throw this country into a constitutional crisis. What would happen if Hillary got elected president and then was indicted for a felony such as perjury, obstruction of justice or intentionally disclosing national security classified information?

The pollsters were having a field day. They were immediately beginning to take fast polls which were showing that Trump was gaining ground while Hillary was losing votes fast. Hillary had a 4 to 8 point lead nationally. The swing states were beginning to get closer as the news spread. The new poll results on Wednesday, November 2, were showing Trump had taken the lead nationally, 46 to 45. The results were also showing Trump leading in the 3 critical states of Florida, Ohio and North Carolina. The Libertarian vote went down by several points from 8 to 2 points with Trump getting these votes instead of Hillary. It appeared that the FBI announcement was having a significant effect on the polling results.

On Friday afternoon, November 4, 2016, FBI Director James Comey announced the FBI had used special equipment to review the emails on the Anthony Wiener and Huma Abedin's computer, and they had found no additional emails that would change the outcome of their investigation. Once again, Hillary was being cleared of wrong doing so she would not be indicted.[50]

The big question remained as to whether the damage had already been done, and was it too late to get this new information out to the voters? It was only 4 days until the election and there was excitement in the air.

---

[50] Information obtained from CNN, MSNBA, Fox News, NBC, CBS and ABC.

CHAPTER 36

Election Night Shock and Awe

November 8, 2016

This race was over and it was time to start the party. Many voters thought that Hillary had won, and it was just a formality to have Election Day so the celebration could begin. Hillary was in New York at the Jacob Javits Center where lots of people gathered so they could party together. Why did so many people feel this way? The polls were showing that Hillary had the lead, although some polls reflected that Trump was gaining. Most polls made it clear that Trump did not have time to overtake her lead. The press confirmed this feeling with many TV stations and the print press confirming that Hillary would win. Even some in the Trump camp were thinking that Trump had done all he could do, but it simply was not enough to win. No one thought that Trump could carry Florida, North Carolina, Ohio, Pennsylvania, Wisconsin, and Michigan. The experts did not think Trump had a pathway to win, because there was no way he could win all of these states, maybe some, but certainly not all of them. Trump had threatened to spend a lot of time in California, but in the last few days he decided to stay in the Eastern part of the country while Hillary, fearing that Trump might try to take California, decided to spend extra time in her favorite state. Hillary's campaign managers thought Trump was *wasting his time trying to carry all the eastern block of states mentioned above.*

The evening started off as predicted. The southeastern part of the country in the Eastern time zone would report first because their polls closed earlier than in the Central time zone. The South was Trump country so no one was surprised that Tennessee, Alabama, Mississippi, Arkansas,

Kentucky, Louisiana and Georgia went for Trump. The experts figured there were six states critical to both candidates: Florida, Ohio, Iowa, Michigan, Wisconsin and Pennsylvania. The big surprise came when Florida went for Trump. The Hillary camp had thought Florida would go for her because the polls and press predicted a win for her. So what happened?

I live in Florida and everywhere I went I tried to talk about the race. I can confirm that many voters secretly told me they were going to vote for Trump. They did not want to say so publicly but confided in me how they felt. Some were upset at the alleged corruption in the Clinton Foundation while others thought she should have been indicted for mishandling classified national security information on her private server. Many of the people I talked to did not especially like some of the Trump statements and some of his conduct, but they wanted a change and they thought Hillary would simply carry on the Obama policies. For example, Obamacare was not working. The premiums were out of control and the deductibles were more than they could afford. It was like having no insurance at all.

The silent voters in Florida became silent no longer, and the news media began to wonder what was going on in the country. What was happening in Florida was also going on in the other critical states, and the news media began to get a look at the electoral votes rather than the popular votes. This is just what Kellyanne Conway had planned for the winning combination of states to get the necessary 270 electoral votes.

One by one the critical states began to report, and the mood began to change. Now, for the first time, the news media began to look for a pathway for Hillary to win. It was not who was winning the popular vote that now mattered, but the electoral vote that was going to control the outcome. The Hillary celebration crowd began to leave the Javits Center, and, the longer the night went on, the sadder the picture became for Hillary as Trump's Electoral College numbers began to increase to the magical 270 mark. Rather than the election being called at 9 p.m., it was about 2:40 a.m. the next morning that Trump was declared the winner and became the President Elect of the United States. We found out just how upset the people were at Hillary and the Democratic platform, and how much they wanted a change in the direction the country was going.[51]

---

[51] Information furnished by Fox News Network

CHAPTER 37

Breaking News

Hillary Elected President of California

Trump Elected President of the United States of America

Should We Abolish the Electoral College?

Some people believe we should elect our president based only on the popular vote. They say the Electoral College is outdated and no longer needed.

All of our presidential elections since 1804 have been governed by the Twelfth Amendment to the United States Constitution which provides the procedure for the election of the president and vice president of the United States. This amendment modified and updated Article II Section I of our original constitution of 1789.

The main purpose of the Electoral College is three fold:

1. To prevent a more populated state from having more power over a less populated state.
2. To prevent the coastal regions of our country in 1789 from having more power over the interior parts of our country.
3. To prevent the Northern region of our country from having more power over the Southern region of our country.

Today many believe that reason number one, stated above, still remains the most important factor for the existence of the Electoral College, which prevents a more populated state from having more power over a less populated state. Let's take a more detailed look at this situation and see if we agree.

Trump won the popular vote in 31 states. Hillary won 19 states and The District of Columbia. He got 62% of the total number of states compared to Hillary's 38%.

Hillary won California with 5,860,714 votes to Trump's 3,151,821 votes or 61.6% to 33.1%, exclusive of the other candidates. Thus, one state, California, gave Hillary the popular vote lead for the entire nation. But, deduct her California vote from her national vote leaving her with 54,978,783 and deduct Trump's California vote from his national vote leaving him with 57,113,976. He wins in the other 49 states, 51.3% to her 48.7%. [52]Never has a candidate won the national popular vote and yet received so few Electoral College votes as did Hillary in this election.[53]

So, now you see why it is proper to say that Hillary was elected President of California and Trump was elected President of the United States.

This exemplifies the wisdom of the Electoral College. It prevents the vote of any one state's population from overriding the vote of the others. Kellyanne Conway, an expert in polling and Trump's campaign manager, saw this early in the election process. She devised her strategy to win the election with 7 pathways to the White House when all the so called experts reported there was almost no pathway to a Trump victory. Conway ignored California with its huge Democratic majority and went after the 7 states that would give Trump the necessary electoral votes to win: Florida, North Carolina, Michigan, Pennsylvania, Ohio, Iowa and Wisconsin. Thus, the Electoral College is working exactly as our Founding Fathers intended.

Therefore, we must ask: "Should one or two of our more populated states be able to control who wins the presidency?"

---

[52] *BuzzFeed* was the source of this information.

[53] Fox News, "Fox & Friends," May 3, 2017.

CHAPTER 38

The Final Analysis

The Silent Voters Speak

"With a Quiet Voice Becoming a Loud Chorus"[54]

The Finest Politician Money Couldn't Buy?

We have just completed one of the most historic elections in the history of our country. Never has a major political party nominated a woman to be president. Even more unusual is the fact that Charles Ortel of World Net Daily had reported in October, 2015, that Bill and Hillary Clinton were involved in criminal activity for alleged corruption in the use of their Clinton Foundation activities, aka pay to play. Just prior to her nomination, the FBI had reported that Hillary would not be indicted for use of her private server in negligently handling classified information. Many people disagreed with this decision.

Her Democratic Party opponent, Bernie Sanders, was an Independent U.S. Senator from Vermont running as a Democratic Socialist.

Regarding the other party, never have we had 17 candidates running for the top spot on the ticket. Even more unusual is the fact that Donald Trump promised he would self- fund his campaign and accept no contributions from lobbyists, the super rich or political action committees, PAC's. This meant that

---

[54] This quote was taken from a speech delivered by President Donald Trump after he was elected President.

no one could buy his influence. Many believe that our politicians have been bought by special interest, lobbyists and PAC's. Trump campaigned on the idea that lobbyists would be banned. When Donald Trump first announced his candidacy, no one took him seriously. Many thought he would drop out of the race within a short time rather than spend his own money to fund a serious run for the presidency. The political experts considered him a joke. He had never run for any political office. Who did he think he was kidding, running for President of the United States in his first attempt at politics?

President Obama assured the American public that Hillary was eminently qualified to hold the office and that she had done nothing wrong that would merit a federal indictment much less a conviction. This position was affirmed when FBI Director James Comey announced that the FBI would not recommend an indictment of Hillary even though she had seriously mishandled classified national security information by using an unprotected private server not approved by the State Department. The FBI said she was grossly negligent in her dealings with top secret and classified information. Comey confirmed that when Hillary told Congress she had never sent or received classified information on her private server that that statement was not true and they had found many examples of top secret or classified information being used on her private server. Many were asking, "Why wasn't Hillary indicted?" Could it be that Trump was correct when he said the election was rigged against him? It was reported that Attorney General Lynch refused to impanel a Grand Jury and/ or President Obama had ordered her to make sure Hillary was not indicted. This was after she met privately with Bill Clinton at the airport in Phoenix, Arizona, at the time Bill Clinton was also under FBI investigation for his part in the alleged corruption of the Clinton Foundation. It was later reported that General Lynch was being considered for reappointment to the Attorney General position if Hillary won. Was there a deal that Lynch would not indict Hillary and Hillary would reappoint Lynch as Attorney General when Hillary won? Could it be that Director James Comey decided to hold a press conference in which he tried to explain in detail why Hillary was not indicted and why he later wrote a letter to Congress reopening the investigation after more emails were found on Huma Abedin and Anthony Weiner's computer? Was he trying to warn the people that Hillary should have been indicted? Remember, the FBI can only investigate crimes and cannot impanel a Grand Jury.

While all of this chaos was going on, Trump was fighting his own battles.

Tapes were played which revealed that Trump said he could make inappropriate advances toward women because he was rich and famous. Many women came forward alleging that he had kissed and groped them without their consent. Eleven women alleged that he sexually assaulted them, the last one being Jessica Drake, a porn star who said he offered her $10,000 for a private meeting with him. Trump denied these allegations. He made disparaging remarks about women, Mexicans, Muslims and gays. He threatened to build a wall along our Southern border to keep out illegal immigrants. Veterans got upset that he refused to call John McCain a war hero simply because he was shot down and captured. After all of this came out, many people refused to support him including some women, the Republican Party, the Washington establishment and many veterans. Trump's insults and put-downs of his Republican opponents and later Hillary were extreme, consistent and legendary. Voters were shocked and disappointed at the rhetoric, though others thought it might take this to make needed changes. Many of the Republican candidates refused to support Trump, even though they had signed a pledge agreeing to support the Republican nominee.

As the day of the election came closer, many polls showed Hillary with a 3-5 point lead and a few predicted an 8% to 10% point win. The media said the race was already over and Hillary planned for a large party. The experts said the race would be called by 9 p.m. as Hillary was going to run away with a substantial lead. Many people in the Trump camp believed Trump was going to lose and many supporters began to doubt his ability to win the election. His path to victory was difficult, if not impossible, to achieve. It was thought he could not win Florida, North Carolina, Ohio, Michigan, Wisconsin, Pennsylvania and Iowa. Yet, many people in these states quietly and secretly decided to vote for Trump without revealing their preference until the day of the election.

Election night results were shocking to many. Why did Hillary lose? Did she lose because Comey's action politically indicted her? Many voters felt she was dishonest in lying to Congress, that she should have been indicted for her reckless handling of top secret information, and that she mishandled the Clinton Foundation by requiring a donation from anyone wanting to meet with her as Secretary of State? She had promised to continue Obamacare and many other Obama policies when the voters felt it was time for a change. In regard to the released emails from Russia, it was rumored that the Clintons tried to discredit Putin when Bill was president and Putin felt it was payback time. It appears Putin returned the action by trying to discredit Hillary. Finally, some voters simply did not trust her, and this fact was reinforced by Trump calling her, "Crooked Hillary."

Why did Trump win? Many believed he could not be bought. Trump said he was going to "Make America Great Again," and that struck a chord that won him crowds of thousands who came to his rallies. Trump promised to bring jobs back to America, as many voters had lost their jobs to illegal immigrants and companies were leaving America to build plants in other countries. As usual, the condition of the economy was still a critical factor in this election. Remember the phrase, "It's the economy, stupid." It was applicable in this race also. Trump promised to secure the borders and deport criminal immigrants with terrorist ties. He promised to amend the U.S. Constitution regarding term limits of the members of Congress. Many voters felt the lack of term limits had resulted in much of the corruption present in Washington. He promised to repeal and replace Obamacare with an affordable and workable health care plan at a time when premiums and deductions were too high for most people to pay. In the final analysis, the voters were tired of having politicians who did nothing for the people. It was time for a change and Trump was their only choice. Trump said "drain the swamp" and that caught voters' attention. Trump stated he would make necessary changes to our tax code, reducing business tax to 15% from 35% and also lowering middle income taxes. He promised to restore America's infrastructure which would add jobs. Because of his image of "getting things done," a lot of voters believed him. The silent majority finally spoke with a quiet voice becoming a loud chorus.

We are about to see if Trump can deliver on his promises.

THE END

ABOUT THE AUTHOR

Bill Marks was born and raised in Nashville, Tennessee. After graduating from Montgomery Bell Academy in 1960, he attended The University of Tennessee in Knoxville, receiving a Bachelor of Science degree in Business Administration and a Doctor of Jurisprudence degree from the College of Law where he was awarded The Outstanding Trial Attorney in Moot Court. He received a Masters of Arts degree from Asbury Theological Seminary in Wilmore, Kentucky. At the University of Tennessee, he was selected for membership in Omicron Delta Kappa National Honor Society, Who's Who in American Universities and Colleges, Scarabbean Senior Society and Pledge Master of Pi Kappa Alpha Fraternity.

He was licensed to practice law by The Tennessee Supreme Court in 1967, and practiced law with the firm of Morton, Morton and Lewis in Knoxville for several years, after which he moved to middle Tennessee and established his private law practice. Bill spent many years as a trial lawyer and served as an Assistant District Attorney General for the Seventh Judicial District in the State of Tennessee.

A former president of his local Bar Association and member of The House of Delegates of The Tennessee Bar Association, he was selected for membership in Who's Who Among Lawyers in the South. He held membership in The American Bar Association, Tennessee Bar Association and American Trial Lawyers Association. He was awarded an AV rating, the highest legal and ethical rating by Martindale-Hubble, a lawyer rating system conducted by his peers. He held membership in his local Lions Club and Rotary Club.

Printed in the United States
By Bookmasters